THE CRONICLE HISTORY OF

Henry the fift,

With his battell fought at
Agin Court in *France*.
Togither with *Auntient Pistoll*.

New York London Toronto Sydney Tokyo Singapore

SHAKESPEAREAN ORIGINALS:
FIRST EDITIONS

———

THE CRONICLE HISTORY OF
Henry the fift,
With his battell fought at
Agin Court in *France*.
Togither with *Auntient Pistoll*.

EDITED AND INTRODUCED BY
GRAHAM HOLDERNESS AND BRYAN LOUGHREY

HARVESTER WHEATSHEAF

First published 1993 by
Harvester Wheatsheaf,
Campus 400, Maylands Avenue
Hemel Hempstead
Hertfordshire HP2 7EZ
A division of
Simon & Schuster International Group

Designed by Geoff Green

Typeset in 11pt Bembo
by Photoprint, Torquay, Devon

Printed and bound in Great Britain by
Biddles Ltd, Guildford and King's Lynn

British Library Cataloguing in Publication Data

A catalogue record for this book
is available from the British Library.

ISBN 0–7450–1101–2 (hbk)
ISBN 0–7450–1102–0 (pbk)

---

1 2 3 4 5   97 96 95 94 93

Contents

General Introduction

T H I S series puts into circulation single annotated editions of early modern play-texts whose literary and theatrical histories have been overshadowed by editorial practices dominant since the eighteenth century.

The vast majority of Shakespeare's modern readership encounters his works initially through the standard modernised editions of the major publishing houses, whose texts form the basis of innumerable playhouse productions and classroom discussions. While these textualisations vary considerably in terms of approach and detail, the overwhelming impression they foster is not of diversity but uniformity: the same plays are reprinted in virtually identical words, within a ubiquitous, standardised format. Cumulatively, such texts serve to constitute and define a particular model of Shakespeare's work, conjuring up a body of writing which is given and stable, handed down by the author like holy writ. But the canonical status of these received texts is ultimately dependent not upon a divine creator, but upon those editorial mediations (rendered transparent by the discursive authority of the very texts they ostensibly serve) that shape the manner in which Shakespeare's works are produced and reproduced within contemporary culture.

Many modern readers of Shakespeare, lulled by long-established editorial traditions into an implicit confidence in the object of their attention, probably have little idea of what a sixteenth-century printed play-text actually looked like. Confronted with an example, she or he could be forgiven for recoiling before the intimidating display of linguistic and visual strangeness – antique type, non-standardised spelling, archaic orthographic conventions, unfamiliar and irregular speech prefixes, oddly placed stage directions, and

[1]

General Introduction

possibly an absence of Act and scene divisions. 'It looks more like Chaucer than Shakespeare,' observed one student presented with a facsimile of an Elizabethan text, neatly calling attention to the peculiar elisions through which Shakespeare is accepted as modern, while Chaucer is categorised as ancient. A student reading Chaucer in a modern translation knows that the text is a contemporary version, not a historical document. But the modern translations of Shakespeare which almost universally pass as accurate and authentic representations of an original – the standard editions – offer themselves as simultaneously historical document and accessible modern version – like a tidily restored ancient building.

The earliest versions of Shakespeare's works existed in plural and contested forms. Some nineteen of those plays modern scholars now attribute to Shakespeare (together with the non-dramatic verse) appeared in cheap quarto format during his life, their theatrical provenance clearly marked by an emphasis upon the companies who owned and produced the plays rather than the author.[1] Where rival quartos of a play were printed, these could contrast starkly: the second quarto of *The tragicall historie of Hamlet, prince of Denmarke* (1604), for example, is almost double the length of its first quarto (1603) predecessor and renames many of the leading characters. In 1623, Shakespeare's colleagues Heminges and Condell brought out posthumously the prestigious and expensive First Folio, the earliest collected edition of his dramatic works. This included major works, such as *The Tragedie of Macbeth*, *The Tragedie of Antonie and Cleopatra*, and *The Tempest* which had never before been published. It also contained versions of those plays, with the exception of *Pericles*, which had earlier appeared in quarto, versions which in some cases differ so markedly from their notional predecessors for them to be regarded not simply as variants of a single work, but as discrete textualisations independently framed within a complex and diversified project of cultural production; perhaps, even, in some senses, as separate plays. In the case of *Hamlet*, for example, the Folio includes some eighty lines which are not to be found in the second quarto, yet omits a fragment of around 230 lines which includes Hamlet's final soliloquy,[2] and far greater differences exist between certain other pairings.

This relatively fluid textual situation continued throughout the seventeenth century. Quartos of individual plays continued to appear sporadically, usually amended reprints of earlier editions, but occasionally introducing new works, such as the first publication of Shakespeare and Fletcher's *The two noble kinsmen* (1634), a play which was perhaps excluded from the Folio on the basis of its collaborative status.[3] The title of another work written in collaboration with Fletcher, *Cardenio*, was entered on the Stationer's Register of 1653, but it appears not to have been published and the play is now lost. The First Folio proved a commercial success and was reprinted in 1632, although again amended in detail. In 1663, a third edition appeared which assigned to Shakespeare seven plays, never before printed in folio, viz *Pericles Prince of Tyre; The London prodigall; The history of Thomas Ld Cromwell; Sir John Oldcastle Lord Cobham; The Puritan widow; A Yorkshire tragedy; The tragedy of Locrine*. These attributions, moreover, were accepted uncritically by the 1685 Fourth Folio.

The assumptions underlying seventeenth-century editorial practice, particularly the emphasis that the latest edition corrects and subsumes all earlier editions, is rarely explicitly stated. It is graphically illustrated, though, by the Bodleian Library's decision to sell off as surplus to requirements the copy of the First Folio it had acquired in 1623 as soon as the enlarged 1663 edition came into its possession.[4] Eighteenth-century editors continued to work within this tradition. Rowe set his illustrated critical edition from the 1685 Fourth Folio, introducing further emendations and modernisations. Alexander Pope used Rowe as the basis of his own text, but he 'corrected' this liberally, partly on the basis of variants contained within the twenty-eight quartos he catalogued but more often relying on his own intuitive judgement, maintaining that he was merely 'restoring' Shakespeare to an original purity which had been lost through 'arbitrary Additions, Expunctions, Transpositions of scenes and lines, Confusions of Characters and Persons, wrong application of Speeches, corruptions of innumerable passages'[5] introduced by actors. Although eighteenth-century editors disagreed fiercely over the principles of their task, all of them concurred in finding corruption at every point of textual transmission (and in Capell's case, composition), and sought the restoration of a perceived poetic genius: for Theobald, Warburton, Johnson and Steevens,

[3]

'The multiple sources of corruption justified editorial intervention; in principle at least, the edition that had received the most editorial attention, the most recent edition, was the purest because the most purified.'[6]

This conception of the editorial function was decisively challenged in theory and practice by Edmund Malone, who substituted the principles of archaeology for those of evolution. For Malone, there could be only one role for an editor: to determine what Shakespeare himself had written. Those texts which were closest to Shakespeare in time were therefore the only true authority; the accretions from editorial interference in the years which followed the publication of the First Folio and early quartos had to be stripped away to recover the original. Authenticity, that is, was to be based on restoration understood not as improvement but as rediscovery. The methodology thus offered the possibility that the canon of Shakespeare's works could be established decisively, fixed for all time, by reference to objective, historical criteria. Henceforth, the text of Shakespeare was to be regarded, potentially, as monogenous, derived from a single source, rather than polygenous.

Malone's influence has proved decisive to the history of nineteenth- and twentieth-century bibliographic studies. Despite, however, the enormous growth in knowledge concerning the material processes of Elizabethan and Jacobean book production, the pursuit of Shakespeare's original words sanctioned a paradoxical distrust of precisely those early texts which Malone regarded as the touchstone of authenticity. Many assumed that these texts must themselves have been derived from some kind of authorial manuscript, and the possibility that Shakespeare's papers lay hidden somewhere exercised an insidious fascination upon the antiquarian imagination. Libraries were combed, lofts ransacked, and graves plundered, but the manuscripts have proved obstinately elusive, mute testimony to the low estimate an earlier culture had placed upon them once performance and publication had exhausted their commercial value.

Undeterred, scholars attempted to infer from the evidence of the early printed texts the nature of the manuscript which lay behind them. The fact that the various extant versions differed so considerably from each other posed a problem which could only be partially resolved by the designation of some as 'Bad Quartos', and therefore non-Shakespearean; for even the remaining 'authorised' texts varied between themselves enormously, invariably in terms of detail and often in terms of substance. Recourse to the concept of manuscript authenticity could not resolve the difficulty, for such a manuscript simply does not exist.[7] Faced with apparent textual anarchy, editors sought solace in Platonic idealism: each variant was deemed an imperfect copy of a perfect (if unobtainable) paradigm. Once again, the editor's task was to restore a lost original purity, employing compositor study, collation, conflation and emendation.[8]

Compositor study attempts to identify the working practices of the individuals who set the early quartos and the Folio, and thus differentiate the non-Shakespearean interference, stripping the 'veil of print from a text' and thus attempting 'to recover a number of precise details of the underlying manuscript'.[9] Collation, the critical comparison of different states of a text with a view to establishing the perfect condition of a particular copy, provided systematic classification of textual variations which could be regarded as putative corruptions. Emendation allows the editor to select one of the variations thrown up by collation and impose it upon the reading of the selected control text, or where no previous reading appeared satisfactory, to introduce a correction based upon editorial judgement. Conflation is employed to resolve the larger scale divergences between texts, so that, for example, the Folio *Tragedie of Hamlet, Prince of Denmarke* is often employed as the control text for modern editions of the play, but since it 'lacks' entire passages found only in the second quarto, these are often grafted on to the former to create the fullest 'authoritative' text.

The cuts to the Folio *Hamlet* may reflect, however, not a corruption introduced in the process of transmission, but a deliberate alteration to the text authorised by the dramatist himself. In recent years, the proposition that Shakespeare revised his work and that texts might therefore exist in a variety of forms has attracted considerable support. The most publicised debate has centred on the relationship of the quarto *true chronicle historie of the life and death of king Lear and his three daughters* and the Folio *Tragedie of King Lear*.[10] The editors of the recent Oxford Shakespeare have broken new ground by including both texts in their one-volume edition on the grounds that the *Tragedie* represents an authorial revision of the earlier *historie*, which is sufficiently radical to justify classifying it as a separate play. Wells and Taylor founded their revisionist position upon a recognition of the fact that Shakespeare was primarily a working *dramatist* rather than literary author and that he addressed his play-texts towards a particular audience of theatrical professionals who were expected to flesh out the bare skeleton of the performance script: 'The written text of any such manuscript thus depended upon an unwritten para-text which always accompanied it: an invisible life-support system of stage directions, which Shakespeare could expect his first audience to supply, or which those first readers would expect Shakespeare himself to supply orally.'[11] They are thus more open than many of their predecessors to the possibility that texts reflect their theatrical provenance and therefore that a plurality of authorised texts may exist, at least for certain of the plays.[12] They remain, however, firmly author centred – the invisible life-support system can ultimately always be traced back to the dramatist himself and the plays remain under his parental authority.[13]

What, however, if it were not Shakespeare but the actor Burbage who suggested, or perhaps insisted on, the cuts to *Hamlet*? Would the Folio version of the play become unShakespearean? How would we react if we *knew* that the Clown spoke 'More than is set down' and that his ad libs were recorded? Or that the King's Men sanctioned additions by another dramatist for a Court performance? Or that a particular text recorded not the literary script of a play but its performance script? Of course, in one sense we cannot know these things. But drama, by its very nature, is overdetermined, the product of multiple influences simultaneously operating across a single site of cultural production. Eyewitness accounts of performances of the period suggest something of the provisionality of the scripts Shakespeare provided to his theatrical colleagues:

> After dinner on the 21st of september, at about two o'clock, I went with my companions over the water, and in the strewn roof-house saw the tragedy of the first Emperor Julius with at least fifteen characters very well acted. At the end of the comedy they danced according to their custom with extreme elegance. Two in men's clothes and two in women's gave this performance, in wonderful combination with each other.[14]

This passage offers what can seem a bizarre range of codes; the strewn roof-house, well-acted tragedy, comic aftermath and elegant transvestite dance, hardly correspond to the typology of Shakespearean drama our own culture has appropriated. The Swiss tourist Thomas Platter was in fact fortunate to catch the curious custom of the jig between Caesar and the boy dressed as Caesar's wife, for by 1612 'all Jigs, Rhymes and Dances' after plays had been 'utterly abolished' to prevent 'tumults and outrages whereby His Majesty's Peace is often broke'.[15] Shakespeare, however, is the 'author' of the spectacle Platter witnessed only in an extremely limited sense; in this context the dramatist's surname functions not simply to authenticate a literary masterpiece, but serves as a convenient if misleading shorthand term alluding to the complex material practices of the Elizabethan and Jacobean theatre industry.[16] It is in the latter sense that the term is used in this series.

Modern theoretical perspectives have destabilised the notion of the author as transcendant subject operating outside history and culture. This concept is in any event peculiarly inappropriate when applied to popular drama of the period. It is quite possible that, as Terence Hawkes argues, 'The notion of a single "authoritative" text, immediately expressive of the plenitude of its author's mind and meaning, would have been unfamiliar to Shakespeare, involved as he was in the collaborative enterprise of dramatic production and notoriously unconcerned to preserve in stable form the texts of most of his plays.'[17] The script is, of course, an integral element of drama, but it is by no means the only one. This is obvious in forms of representation, such as film, dependent on technologies which emphasise the role of the *auteur* at the expense of that of the writer. But even in the early modern theatre, dramatic realisation depended not just upon the scriptwriter,[18] but upon actors, entrepreneurs, promptbook keepers, audiences, patrons, etc; in fact, the entire wide range of professional and institutional interests constituting the theatre industry of the period.

Just as the scriptwriter cannot be privileged over all other influences, nor can any single script. It is becoming clear that within Elizabethan and Jacobean culture, around each 'Shakespeare' play there circulated a wide variety of texts, performing different theatrical functions and adopting different shapes in different contexts of production. Any of these contexts may be of interest to the modern reader. The so-called Bad Quartos, for example, are generally marginalised as piratically published versions based upon the memorial reconstructions of the plays by bit-part actors. But even if the theory of memorial reconstruction is correct (and it is considerably more controversial than is generally recognised[19]), these quarto texts would provide a unique window on to the plays as they were originally performed and open up exciting opportunities for contemporary performance.[20] They form part, that is, of a rich diversity of textual variation which is shrouded by those traditional editorial practices which have sought to impose a single, 'ideal' paradigm.

In this series we have sought to build upon the pioneering work of Wells and Taylor, albeit along quite different lines. They argue, for example, that

> The lost manuscripts of Shakespeare's work are not the fiction of an idealist critic, but particular material objects which happen at a particular time to have existed, and at another particular time to have been lost, or to have ceased to exist. Emendation does not seek to construct an ideal text, but rather to restore certain features of a lost material object (that manuscript) by correcting certain apparent deficiencies in a second material object (this printed text) which purports to be a copy of the first. Most readers will find this procedure reasonable enough.[21]

The important emphasis here is on the relative status of the two forms, manuscript and printed text: the object of which we can have direct knowledge, the printed text, is judged to be corrupt by conjectural reference to the object of which we can by definition have no direct knowledge, the uncorrupted (but non-existent) manuscript. This corresponds to no philosophical materialism we have encountered. The editors of *Shakespearean Originals* reject the claim that it is possible to construct a rehabilitated text reflecting a form approximating Shakespeare's artistic vision.[22] Instead we prefer to embrace the early printed texts as authentic material objects, the concrete forms from which all subsequent editions ultimately derive.

We therefore present within this series particular textualisations of plays which are not necessarily canonical or indeed even written

General Introduction

by *William Shakespeare, Gent*, in the traditional sense; but which nevertheless represent important facets of Shakespearean drama. In the same way that we have rejected the underlying principles of traditional editorial practice, we have also approached traditional editorial procedures with extreme caution, preferring to let the texts speak for themselves with a minimum of editorial mediation. We refuse to allow speculative judgements concerning the exact contribution of the various individuals involved in the production of a given text the authority to license alterations to that text, and as a result relegate compositor study and collation[23] to the textual apparatus rather than attempt to incorporate them into the text itself through emendation.

It seems to us that there is in fact no philosophical justification for emendation, which foregrounds the editor at the expense of the text. The distortions introduced by this process are all too readily incorporated into the text as holy writ. Macbeth's famous lines, for example, 'I dare do all that may become a man, / Who dares do more, is none,' on closer inspection turn out to be Rowe's. The Folio reads, 'I dare do all that may become a man, / Who dares no more is none.' There seems to us no pressing reason whatsoever to alter these lines,[24] and we prefer to confine all such editorial speculation to the critical apparatus. The worst form of emendation is conflation. It is now widely recognised that the texts of the *true chronicle historie of king Lear* (1608) and *The Tragedie of King Lear* (1623) differ so markedly that they must be considered as two distinct plays and that the composite *King Lear* which is reproduced in every twentieth-century popular edition of the play is a hybrid which grossly distorts both the originals from which it is derived. We believe that the case of *Lear* is a particularly clear example of a general proposition: that *whenever* distinct textualisations are conflated, the result is a hybrid without independent value. It should therefore go without saying that all the texts in this series are based upon single sources.

The most difficult editorial decisions we have had to face concern the modernisation of these texts. In some senses we have embarked upon a project of textual archaeology and the logic of our position points towards facsimile editions. These, however, are already available in specialist libraries, where they are there marginalised by those processes of cultural change which have rendered them alien and forbidding. Since we wish to challenge the hegemony of standard editions by circulating the texts within this series as widely as possible, we have aimed at 'diplomatic' rather than facsimile status and have modernised those orthographic and printing conventions (such as long s, positional variants of u and v, i and j, ligatures and contractions) which are no longer current and likely to confuse. We do so, however, with some misgiving, recognising that as a result certain possibilities open to the Elizabethan reader are thereby foreclosed. On the other hand, we make no attempt to standardise such features as speech prefixes and *dramatis personae*, or impose conventions derived from naturalism, such as scene divisions and locations, upon the essentially fluid and non-naturalistic medium of the Elizabethan theatre. In order that our own editorial practice should be as open as possible we provide as an appendix a sample of the original text in photographic facsimile. The introductory essay attempts to view the play as a work of art in its own right rather than as an analogue to the received text, pointing towards those recent theoretical formulations which have validated its status and where possible to significant theatrical realisations. Annotation is kept deliberately light, but we do try to point out some of the performance possibilities occluded by traditional editorial mediations.

GRAHAM HOLDERNESS AND BRYAN LOUGHREY

NOTES AND REFERENCES

1. The title page of the popular *Titus Andronicus*, for example, merely records that it was 'Plaide by the Right Honourable the Earle of Darbie, Earle of Pembrooke, and Earle of Sussex their Servants', and not until 1598 was Shakespeare's name attached to a printed version of one of his plays, *Love's Labour's Lost*.

2. For a stimulating discussion of the relationship between the three texts of *Hamlet*, see Steven Urkowitz, '"Well-sayd olde Mole", Burying Three *Hamlets* in Modern Editions', in Georgianna Ziegler (ed.), *Shakespeare Study Today* (New York: AMS Press, 1986), pp. 37–70.

3. In the year of Shakespeare's death Ben Jonson staked a far higher claim for the status of the playwright, bringing out the first ever collected edition of English dramatic texts, *The Workes of Beniamin Jonson*, a care-

fully prepared and expensively produced folio volume. The text of his Roman tragedy *Sejanus*, a play originally written with an unknown collaborator, was carefully revised to preserve the purity of authorial input. See Bryan Loughrey and Graham Holderness, 'Shakespearean Features', in Jean Marsden (ed.), *The Appropriation of Shakespeare: Post-Renaissance Reconstructions of the Works and the Myth* (Hemel Hempstead: Harvester Wheatsheaf, 1991), p. 183.

4. F. Madan and G.M.R. Turbutt (eds), *The Original Bodleian Copy of the First Folio of Shakespeare* (Oxford: Oxford University Press, 1905), p. 5.

5. Cited in D. Nicol Smith, *Eighteenth Century Essays* (Oxford: Oxford University Press, 1963), p. 48.

6. Margareta de Grazia, *Shakespeare Verbatim* (Oxford: Oxford University Press, 1991), p. 62. De Grazia provides the fullest and most stimulating account of the important theoretical issues raised by eighteenth-century editorial practice.

7. Unless the Hand D fragment of 'The Booke of Sir Thomas Moore' (British Library Harleian MS 7368) really is that of Shakespeare. See Stanley Wells and Gary Taylor, *William Shakespeare: A Textual Companion* (Oxford: Oxford University Press, 1987), pp. 461–7.

8. See Margaret de Grazia, 'The essential Shakespeare and the material book', *Textual Practice*, vol. 2, no. 1, spring 1988.

9. Fredson Bowers, 'Textual Criticism', in O.J. Campbell and E.G. Quinn (eds), *The Reader's Encyclopedia of Shakespeare* (New York: Methuen, 1966), p. 869.

10. See, for example, Gary Taylor and Michael Warren (eds), *The Division of the Kingdoms* (Oxford: Oxford University Press, 1983).

11. Stanley Wells and Gary Taylor, *William Shakespeare: A Textual Companion* (Oxford: Oxford University Press, 1987), p. 2.

12. See, for example, Stanley Wells, 'Plural Shakespeare', *Critical Survey*, vol. 1, no. 1, spring 1989.

13. See, for example, *Textual Companion*, p. 69.

14. Thomas Platter, a Swiss physician who visited London in 1599 and recorded his playgoing; cited in *The Reader's Encyclopaedia*, p. 634. For a discussion of this passage see Richard Wilson, *Julius Caesar: A Critical Study* (Harmondsworth: Penguin, 1992), chapter 3.

15. E.K. Chambers, *The Elizabethan Stage* (Oxford: Oxford University Press, 1923), pp. 340–1.

16. The texts of the plays sometimes encode the kind of stage business Platter recorded. The epilogue of *2 Henry IV*, for example, is spoken by a dancer who announces that 'My tongue is weary; when my legs are too, I will bid you good night . . .'

17. Terence Hawkes, *That Shakespeherian Rag* (London, Methuen, 1986), p. 75.

18. For a discussion of Shakespeare's texts as dramatic scripts, see Jonathan Bate, 'Shakespeare's Tragedies as working scripts', *Critical Survey*, vol. 3, no. 2, 1991, pp. 118–27.

19. See, for example, Random Cloud [Randall McCleod], 'The Marriage of Good and Bad Quartos', *Shakespeare Quarterly*, vol. 33, no. 4, 1982 pp. 421–30.

20. See, for example, Bryan Loughrey, 'Q1 in modern performance', in Tom Clayton (ed.), *The 'Hamlet' First Published* (Newark, University of Delaware Press, 1992) and Nicholas Shrimpton, 'Shakespeare Performances in London and Stratford-Upon-Avon, 1984–5', *Shakespeare Survey* 39, pp. 193–7.

21. *Textual Companion*, p. 60.

22. The concept of authorial intention, which has generated so much debate amongst critics, remains curiously unexamined within the field of textual studies.

23. Charlton Hinman's Norton Facsimile of *The First Folio of Shakespeare* offers a striking illustration of why this should be so. Hinman set out to reproduce the text of the original First Folio, but his collation of the Folger Library's numerous copies demonstrated that 'every copy of the finished book shows a mixture of early and late states of the text that is peculiar to it alone'. He therefore selected from the various editions those pages he believed represented the printer's final intentions and bound these together to produce something which 'has hitherto been only a theoretical entity, an abstraction: *the* First Folio'. Thus the technology which would have allowed him to produce a literal facsimile in fact is deployed to create an ahistorical composite which differs in substance from every single original upon which it is based. See Charlton Hinman, *The First Folio of Shakespeare* (New York, 1968), pp. xxiii–xxiv.

24. Once the process begins, it becomes impossible to adjudicate between rival conjectural emendations. In this case, for example, Hunter's suggestion that Lady Macbeth should be given the second of these lines seems to us neither more nor less persuasive than Rowe's.

Introduction

T h e Cronicle History of Henry the fift (1600) is an extremely good play. Although radically different from its better known counterpart *The Life of Henry the Fift*, first published in 1623 as part of the 'First Folio' edition of Shakespeare's plays, the earlier text has always existed in the shadow of the later: a 'Bad Quarto', illegitimately recorded from performance or incompetently recollected from memories of performance; a badly printed, abridged and censored version of Shakespeare's 'true originall copie'. As a printed text, the 1600 play has never received any critical consideration beyond its relationship with the later version; and unlike other Quarto plays included in this series – *The Tragicall Historie of Hamlet Prince of Denmarke*, or *The Taming of A Shrew* – *The Cronicle History of Henry the fift* has no independent stage history, having never to our knowledge been performed since the seventeenth century. *Shakespearean Originals* thus brings to public attention what is in essence virtually a new play, carrying none of the interpretative and theatrical baggage accumulated by centuries of critical and production history. For the first time since the historical moment of its original production, as text and performance, *The Cronicle History of Henry the fift* can be addressed in its own right as a vigorous and powerful instance of Elizabethan comic–historical drama.

★

As with the other so-called 'Bad Quartos', *The Cronicle History of Henry the fift* has been interpreted in three ways: as an early draft, later revised by Shakespeare into the Folio text; as an inaccurate documentation, either from observation or memory, of a performance of the Folio text; or as an accurate record of an abridged production of that same text. The first opinion, initiated by scholars such as Pope and Johnson, assumes that the play existed and was produced in the form given here, before being expanded and revised into *The Life of Henry the Fift*. The second, deriving from editors such as Capell and Steevens, assumes that the Folio version represents the 'original', that the play was produced from that text, and that the Quarto represents not an abridged version, but an incomplete record of the complete text. The view that the Quarto partially and inaccurately records a performance of the Folio text was developed and established by G.I. Duthie, the modern progenitor of much 'Bad Quarto' theory: 'the condition of the Q text suggests that it is a memorial reconstruction made by actors who had taken part in performances of F or of a stage version based on F'.[1]

Modern scholars are generally of the opinion that the Quarto is an accurate record of an abridged text used in provincial performance. The editor of the Arden Shakespeare text, J.H. Walter, uses both the memorial reconstruction and the abridgement theories: identifying *The Cronicle History of Henry the fift* as a memorially reconstructed 'Bad Quarto' – 'that is, a corrupt version of the play presumably concocted by one or two members of the company from memory';[2] and then neatly placing the Quarto text by a succinct series of terms of limitation: 'In brief, the Q version may well be based on a cut form of the play used by the company for a reduced cast on tour in the provinces.'[3] 'Brief, based, cut, reduced, provinces' – in one short sentence is assembled a whole vocabulary of strategic marginalisation. The Quarto is everything that the Folio is not: 'based' (both derivative and degraded), not authentic; 'cut', not whole; 'reduced', not entire; 'provincial' rather than metropolitan.

Gary Taylor in the individual Oxford Shakespeare edition follows this line of interpretation, concluding that the Quarto represents an actual performance-text, but not one authorised directly by Shakespeare. The Folio text 'shows every sign of having been printed directly from "foul papers" ' (i.e. of derivation from a manuscript source); while a combination of 'extraordinary features' of the Quarto text – abridgement, significant exclusions, verbal variation, a pervasive textual 'corruption' and a penchant for 'nonsense' –

'seems explicable only upon the assumption that Q is the result of a reconstruction by memory of the play as performed – as performed, moreover, in a severely abridged and adapted text, such as might have been used by a troupe of actors touring the provinces'.[4] On this basis Taylor confidently discredits the Quarto as a printed text: 'certainly the bulk of the readings in which it differs from F have no claim whatsoever on our attention';[5] though in the same paragraph he describes the same text as 'an historical document of far more authority than the hypotheses of any twentieth century scholar'.[6] These assertions are not as self-contradictory as they appear, since Taylor's evaluation of the Quarto differentiates its status as a record of performance ('a transcript of the text of Shakespeare's play by two men whose living depended on their memories, and who had acted in *Henry V* within a year or so of its first performance',[7]) from its status as an embodiment of the author's 'intentions'. This even-handed justice is, however, immediately thrown off balance if it is recognised that both the memorial reconstruction and the abridgement theories are scholarly hypotheses with far less claim on our attention than the authority of a historical document such as *The Cronicle History of Henry the fift*.

Comparative evaluation between Quarto and Folio texts, the invariable practice of modern scholarship and criticism, has concentrated on the quality of the text and on the significance of its apparent omissions. The first of these concerns can be addressed relatively simply. *The Cronicle History of Henry the fift* has hardly been regarded as anything other than a 'bad' text. Use of the term 'Bad Quarto' to identify a dramatic text supposedly reported or reconstructed from a theatrical performance permits a pervasive strategic dispersion of the attribution of 'badness', from a description of a particular mode of transmission (illegitimately copied from performance or from the memory of performance, rather than derived from some supposedly more authoritative source such as authorial manuscript, a scribal copy of the MS, or an authorially 'approved' prompt-copy) to ascriptions of artistic or even moral 'badness' on the part of both the text and its conjectural producers. Just as ostensibly innocent bibliographical terms such as 'corruption' and 'contamination' carry far too strong a charge of ethical evaluation for their signifying power to operate purely at the level of objective scholarship, so a 'Bad Quarto' can readily be received as not only bad in itself, but the product of bad men, the unscrupulous Elizabethan 'pirate', the ubiquitous 'playhouse thief'.

Consider how confidently G.I. Duthie identifies as 'nonsense' a piece of perfectly intelligible dramatic writing, Flewellen's speech at the siege:

> *Flew.*   . . . there is an Ensigne
> There, I do not know how you call him, but by Jesus I think
> He is as valiant a man as *Marke Anthonie*, he doth maintain
> the bridge most gallantly: yet he is a man of no reckoning:
> But I did see him do gallant service.
> *Gover.* How do you call him?
> *Flew.* His name is ancient *Pistoll*

(This edition, p. 57)

Why, asks Duthie, does Flewellen contradict himself over his knowledge of Pistoll's name? The obvious answer is memorial reconstruction: 'I do not think we could comfortably attribute this ineptitude to Shakespeare even in a first draft, whereas on the other hand it may well have been brought about through memorial confusion'.[8] Has Duthie forgotten, we might well ask, by some osmosis of amnesia, that spasmodic absent-mindedness is Flewellen's key character-trait, or rather one of the main running gags supporting his comic role?

> *Flew.* Captain *Gower*, what call you the place where Alexander
> the big was borne? . . .   (p. 73)
>
> . . . the Rivers name at *Monmorth*,
> Is called Wye.
> But tis out of my braine, what is the name of the other . . . (p. 74)
>
> . . . our King being in his ripe
> Wits and judgements, is turne away, the fat knite
> With the great belly doublet: I am forget his name.   (p. 74)

In fact Duthie's knowledge of the text was as secure as usual, and he goes on to quote these same examples. His argument, however, is that the forgetting of Pistoll's name is not a consistency of comic role, but an 'anticipation' of the subsequent scenes! 'The reporter has confused this scene with IV vii. There, in the passage from line 22 on (F numbering), Fluellen, in both Q and F, twice declares that he has forgotten a name.'⁹ In this way the groundless hypothesis of memorial reconstruction is allowed to override what would otherwise be an obvious consistency in the treatment of Flewellen's character.

Gary Taylor, who as we have seen goes some way towards acknowledging the Quarto's authority, and incorporates selective readings from it into his edition, loyally follows Duthie with the same charge of nonsense, inveighing with the full armoury of bibliographical rhetoric against the text's 'corruption':

> It is difficult to deny that Q is far more frequently and seriously corrupt than F. One need not submit to the draconian metrical legislation of Pope in order to recognize that Q far more frequently and awkwardly departs from the decasyllabic five-stress line which, with certain standard variations, constitutes the norm of Shakespearean verse. That Q on occasion prints nonsense need not surprise us; but the quality of the nonsense bespeaks some extraordinary agency of corruption.¹⁰

Taylor's example is a passage from the Bishop's speech on the Salic Law:

> The Archbishop of Canterbury's disquisition on the Salic Law provides a particularly compelling example of [corruption], because the speech in F clearly derives from its counterpart in Raphael Holinshed's *Chronicles*, and F's version in turn clearly underlies the nonsense printed in Q:

> > Hugh Capet also, that usurped the crown,
> > To fine his title with some show of truth,
> > When in pure truth it was corrupt and naught,
> > Conveyed himself as heir to the Lady Inger,
> > Daughter to Charles, the foresaid Duke of Lorraine;
> > So that, as clear as is the summer's sun,
> > King Pepin's title and Hugh Capet's claim,
> > King Charles his satisfaction all appear
> > To hold in right and title of the female.

> The Lady Lingard was the daughter of Charlemain, not Charles the

Duke of Lorraine; 'the foresaid Duke of Lorraine' has not in fact
been mentioned at all; nor has King Pepin; nor has King Charles
. . .[11]

The Folio version of this speech is as follows:[12]

King *Pepin*, which deposed *Childerike*,
Did as Heire Generall, being descended
Of *Blithild*, which was the daughter to King *Clothair*,
Make Clayme and Title to the Crowne of France,
Hugh Capet also, who vsurpt the Crowne
Of *Charles* the Duke of Loraine, sole Heire male
Of the true line and stock of Charles the Great:
To find his Title with some shewes of truth,
Though in pure truth it was corrupt and naught,
Conuey'd himselfe as th'Heire to th'Lady *Lingare*,
Daughter to *Charlemaine*, who was the Sonne
To *Lewes* the Emperor, and *Lewes* the Sonne
Of *Charles* the Great: also King *Lewes* the Tenth,
Who was sole Heire to the Vsurper *Capet*,
Could not keepe quiet in his conscience,
Wearing the Crowne of France, 'till satisfied,
That faire Queene *Isabel*, his Grandmother,
Was Lineall of the Lady *Ermengare*,
Daughter to *Charles* the foresaid Duke of Loraine:
By the which Marriage, the Lyne of *Charles* the Great
Was re-vnited to the Crowne of France.
So that as clear as is the Summers Sunne,
King *Pepins* Title, and *Hugh Capets* Clayme,
King *Lewes* his satisfaction, all appeare
To hold in Right and Title of the Female:
So doe the Kings of France vnto this day.

The Folio text certainly gives more of Holinshed's narrative than
the Quarto: but in point of historical accuracy, it is not without its
own oddities. 'Charlemaine' and 'Charles the Great' appear here as
two separate people, when in fact, of course, they were one and
the same. The Lady 'Lingare' ('Inger' in Q, corrected to 'Lingard'
in modern editions) was actually the daughter of Charles the Bald,
not Charles the Great, who appears here as his own grandfather.
Baldness and greatness are known to co-exist (as in the case of
Shakespeare himself): but that is no reason for confusing these

attributes. The confusion was, on the other hand, well established and of considerable authority, since it appears in Holinshed: 'the Lady Lingard, daughter to King Charlemaine, son to Lewes the emperor, that was son to Charles the Great'.[13]

The Folio text thus stands immediately accused of 'nonsense'. So too, though, to be fair, does the common source of both texts, Holinshed's *Chronicles*. 'King *Lewes* the Tenth', for example, was really King Louis IX. The error was made by Holinshed in copying from his primary source, Edward Halle's *Union of the Two Noble and Illustre Famelies of Lancaster and York*. Another symptom of the Quarto's propensity for 'nonsense' is the fact that in place of this same Louis is substituted the name of the current French king, Charles:

> King *Charles* his satisfaction all appeare,
> To hold in right and title of the female . . .
>
> (This edition, p. 38)

In both Holinshed and the Folio text, the reference is clearly to King Louis' concern with the lineage of his grandmother, about which he demands to be 'satisfied'. The Quarto text, however, (whether copying from the Folio, from Holinshed or from some other source) omits the passage dealing with that claim, and jumps straight from the Lady Inger to the lines which in F and Holinshed concern the Lady Ermengare. Thus where both Holinshed and F add to the emphasis on King Louis' claim to legitimacy, a reference to subsequent French kings – 'So doe the Kings of France vnto this day' – Q substitutes the name of the current French king, Charles, in order to stress that the claim through the female line is all that sustains the incumbent French monarchy.

Since, however, the Folio text could not tell the difference between Charlemaine and Charles the Great; and since Holinshed could not tell the difference between Louis the Tenth and Louis IX; it is perhaps assuming too much to expect the Quarto to distinguish between the Lady Lingare and the Lady Ermengare. One woman's name sufficed to make the dramatic point about female succession.

Taylor simply assumes that the Folio text, with its more accurate, extensive and literal copying from Holinshed, necessarily constitutes the more authentic, more Shakespearean of the two versions. That may be a reasonable assumption. Equally reasonable would be the contrary assumption, that in the Folio we find a medium of slavish, unimaginative versification unexemplified anywhere else in the play; and that in the Quarto we find the work of a dramatist or scriptwriter who has pared down and refined the historical trivia of Holinshed to a single, unmistakable dramatic effect. Historical accuracy is hardly a strong point in any of the available texts. It should therefore be possible to compare them in terms of their dramatic and poetic values, rather than by their supposed fidelity to some putative original source.

It is necessary then to suspend the 'Bad Quarto' nomenclature and to look directly at the text, in terms both of its intrinsic characteristics and its differences from the Folio version. Before doing so, however, it is necessary to consider another, related argument, which is that the Quarto text represents not just a memorially reconstructed and abridged version of F, but a *censored* version of the play. The significance of 'omissions' (i.e. passages that appear in one text and not another) varies from one theoretical context to another. The very concept of 'omission', of course, presupposes that the shorter text is a reduced version of the longer. The memorial reconstruction theory tends to assume that 'omissions' derived from lapses of memory, or from the pirate-actors remembering more accurately their own parts and the scenes in which they played a substantial role. 'Abridgement' theory assumes that omissions arise simply through the process of cutting to reduce the running time: again, the effects would be fairly arbitrary, depending on nothing more critical than the question of who made the cuts. It has been extensively argued that the differences between Q and F constitute highly significant omissions of particular types of material. Taylor argues:

> The text actually printed in 1600 . . . omits, from the play as we know it, the opening scene (with its revelation of mixed ecclesiastical motives for supporting Henry's claim to France), lines 115–35 of 1.2 (which culminate in the Archbishop's offer of church financing for the war), all reference in 2.1 to Henry's personal responsibility for Falstaff's condition, Cambridge's hint of motives other than simple bribery for the conspiracy against Henry (2.2.154–9), the bloodthirsty MacMorris and most of Henry's savage ultimatum in 3.3, all of

Burgundy's description of the devastation Henry has wreaked on France (5.2.38–62). Whoever was responsible for them, the effect of the differences between this text and the one printed in all modern editions is to remove almost every difficulty in the way of an unambiguously patriotic interpretation of Henry and his war – that is, every departure from the kind of play which theatrical convention and the national mood would have led audiences of 1599 to expect.[14]

Taylor's suggestion is that initial performances of the play, using the Folio text, must have disappointed patriotic expectation, leading to an abridgement which carefully omitted every obstacle standing in the way of such an interpretation.

Annabel Patterson[15] has pursued this line of argument in more historical detail, proposing that the Quarto text displays an illuminating relationship with the political conflicts of the period 1599–1601. The 1600 text seems to Patterson a much more straightforward, unambiguously patriotic play, a drama which would seem in its ideological orthodoxy and political loyalty to answer quite readily to the patriotic interpretations of Tillyard and Lily B. Campbell. The longer version in the Folio seems by contrast a much more ambiguous text, offering a liberal and possibly even dangerous range of political commentary on the immediate historical context of its production. The Quarto seems to pull back from the incendiary political conflicts (involving especially the Earl of Essex) into which the fuller version, for whatever reason, seems to have intervened. Particularly dangerous must have been the fifth Chorus of the Folio version, with its coded reference to Essex returning in triumph from his Irish expedition.

In 1600, then, the fifth Chorus was so ambiguous that Shakespeare's company . . . could not have risked giving it the publicity of print, where its textual instabilities would be fully open to inspection. It brought down with it, presumably, the rest of the Choruses, including those whose message might well have enhanced the simple patriotism of the Quarto text as a whole. What Shakespeare intended by creating this dangerous instability in the first place is another question altogether . . .[16]

Clearly this line of interpretation brings the Quarto text into consideration, where most critical and scholarly approaches would exclude it. Annabel Patterson is interested in the different texts as exemplifying different kinds of historical intervention into contemporary politics: she is not at all concerned with value-judgements discriminating one text from another in terms of literary quality. None the less, this theoretical approach could easily be seen as an extension of the 'Bad Quarto' theory, since it argues that the fuller text contains a much greater potentiality for subversion; and that the shorter text is reduced to strict conformity with the political and ideological orthodoxy of the day. The Quarto text, it could then be argued, is of 'merely' historical interest; and it is from the Folio text that modern criticism derives its interpretation of the play as a critical and subversive interrogation of monarchy, imperialism, heroism and war. It is certainly the case that those many modern readings of *The Life of Henry the Fift* that have found possibilities of subversion in the play have focused on the device of the Chorus and on some of the speeches and scenes not to be found in the 1600 Quarto text.[17]

Once again, however, the scope of interpretation is tightly restricted by the traditional scholarly and critical insistence on comparative analysis. The Quarto is always read in relation to the Folio: either, in the 'Bad Quarto' approach, as exemplifying a quality of badness measurable by the demonstrable goodness of the more familiar text; or as constituted not by its own characteristic dramatic structure and poetic texture, but by those passages in the Folio text for which the Quarto contains no equivalent. Since the Folio text is longer and larger than the Quarto, containing all its dramatic action augmented by additional scenes, longer passages and the device of the Chorus, it is quite reasonable to assume that the Quarto is an abridged version of the Folio. As there is no direct evidence for this view, it is just as possible that the Folio is an expanded version of the Quarto.

The present edition of *The Cronicle History of Henry the fift* makes no attempt to arbitrate in that dispute. Its purpose is not to advance new or revised arguments about the relations between the two texts; but partly to dissociate Quarto from Folio so as to view the earlier text in its own right as an independent cultural object; and partly to essay comparisons between Quarto and Folio on the assumption of textual multiplicity and equivalence, as distinct from the tradition of interpretation predicated on the Quarto's self-evident inferiority. In a hierarchical configuration of texts separated by principles of moral discrimination, priority is automatically given to the readings of the texts adjudged 'good'. On a level playing-field of textual plurality, variant readings can be objectively compared and apprehended as different from one another, without any establishing of discursive hierarchy. As Stephen Urkowitz has pointed out, the 'memorial reconstruction' hypothesis itself

> seems to have prevented close examination of the fundamental documents of our literary-dramatic tradition by its practitioners, teachers of literature and performers of plays. Labeling certain texts as 'bad' quartos has removed them from the normal discourse in which such documents would otherwise be included.[18]

Although Urkowitz leans, like Stanley Wells and Gary Taylor, towards a view of the multiple texts as indications of authorial revision – thus clinging to an umbilical cord firmly attaching the texts to an 'author' – his key emphasis is surely correct. The various surviving printed texts of early modern drama should be accepted as the 'fundamental documents', and should be 'studied for what they are, in and of themselves, rather than solely as pernicious desecrations of Shakespeare's iconic originals'.[19]

It is first necessary to identify the play's genre and conventions. *The Life of Henry the Fift* is remarkable particularly for its introduction of the Chorus, that distancing epic device designed both to bring the events of history into dramatic immediacy, and to estrange them into epic remoteness. In other respects it adheres to the dramatic structure developed for the historical drama in the *Henry IV* plays: with long 'serious' scenes of political and military action, intercut with shorter scenes of comic parody and travesty. One critical element in this latter relationship is the absence of Falstaff, whose participation in *The Life of Henry the Fift* was projected at the end of *The Second Part of King Henry the Fourth*, but who figures in *The Life of Henry the Fift* only through the reporting of his death. Critical opinion has dwelt on this non-appearance of a great comic character, and read that absence as symptomatic of a movement away from comedy towards the epic and historical. It is certainly true that the Falstaffian comic function performed by the remaining tavern-companions, Pistoll, Bardolfe and Nym, is substantially reduced in *The Life of Henry the Fift* by comparison with the *Henry IV* plays. It is equally apparent, though never acknowledged, that this diminution applies less strongly to the Quarto text, which generally presents shorter versions of the 'serious' scenes, and thereby gives a correspondingly greater prominence – despite the absence of the Scottish and Irish captains – to the comic scenes involving Pistoll and Bardolfe, Gower and Flewellen.

That deflection of the play towards the comic mode affects both 'serious' and 'comic' passages alike. We are accustomed to thinking of the portrayal of Henry in this play as closely aligned to that aloof and fastidious figure who at the end of *The Second Part of King Henry the Fourth* formally renounces his comic heritage along with his low-life companions. The King Henry of *The Cronicle History* more closely resembles the Prince Hal of the Eastcheap scenes in those earlier plays. The genre of the Elizabethan history play was an eclectic form, containing many plays in which the new historical style, based on a close relationship with the Tudor chronicles, interacted with older modes, with the conventions of romance and the manners of comedy. In such plays the historical drama reveals itself as very much a popular genre, often acknowledging by its themes and situations an origin on the public stages of citizen London. Where tragic history plays like *Richard II* restrict the dramatic action to authentic historical events and characters, the comic history maintained a freedom to invent actions and situations without precedent, or even quite unthinkable, in written history. Its sources were less the written chronicles, more materials from a still largely oral popular culture – ballads, romances, folk-tales, fairy-stories. It represents an older kind of history, still indeed visible in the Tudor chronicles, in which the rich and varied fantasy worlds of myth and legend consort with the new positivism of historical narrative.

In historical medleys such as *James IV* and *Edward I*, historical characters mingle with citizens and figures of legend such as Robin Hood. It was in fact this genre that produced the dominant tradition for the dramatic representation of Henry V: a comic tradition, in which the king's 'riotous youth' is used positively as a way of humanising the monarch. This king is not so much the epic hero of Agincourt as the good fellow of Eastcheap; not the mirror of all Christian kings, but the prince of carnival. In Dekker's *The Shoemaker's Holiday* (1599), a carnival play based on the London apprentices' Shrove Tuesday saturnalia, Henry V appears as a 'bully king' who associates freely with citizens and apprentices, dispenses justice and equality, resolves conflict and promotes harmony. The king does not pose as a common man, as does Henry in the *Henry V* plays on the night before Agincourt. The main source for the *Henry IV* and *Henry V* plays, the anonymous *Famous Victories of Henry the Fifth*, is distinguished by its predominantly comic mode.

Each scene in which the king or his representatives appear in *The Cronicle History of Henry the fift* is very largely concerned with the enactment of some kind of game, role-play, trickery, deception or practical joke. The play begins with an action already in process – 'Shall I call in Thambassadors my Liege' – and Henry holds up that action to debate the legitimacy of the war. Although certainly long for a parenthesis, that debate is essentially a pause before the action continues with the entry of the Dolphin's Ambassadors. The main business of the scene is thus the mocking gift of the tennis balls. Each scene involving Henry is in a similar way centred on a particular game: the grim practical joke on Cambridge, Masham and Gray; Exeter's returning of the Dolphin's mockery; the king's disguising himself as a common man on the night before Agincourt, his deception of the soldier Williams and the staged quarrel with Flewellen, and his wooing of the French princess. Of course, all these examples are common to the two texts: but in the Quarto the comic behaviour of the king is much more clearly and consistently in focus, unimpeded by the historicising rhetoric of the Folio's Chorus. That part of the dramatic action representing the siege of Harfleur, which in *The Life of Henry the Fift* fills most of an 'act' – beginning with the Chorus's description of the siege, followed by Henry's famous 'Once more vnto the Breach, / Deare friends' address to his troops, and ending with the long and particularly brutal speech of threatening to the citizens of Harfleur, appears in the Quarto pared down to a simple exercise in bluffing:

> *King.* How yet resolves the Governour of the Towne?
> This is the latest parley weele admit:

Therefore to our best mercie give your selves,
Or like to men proud of destruction, defie us to our worst,
For as I am a souldier, a name that in my thoughts
Becomes me best, if we begin the battery once againe,
I will not leave the halfe atchieved Harflew,
Till in her ashes she be buried,
The gates of mercie are all shut up.
What say you, will you yeeld and this avoyd,
Or guiltie in defence be thus destroyd?

(p. 55)

The distinction between Quarto and Folio here cannot focus simply on what is there in one and absent in the other. The differences amount to a clear distinction of genre: the Folio epic and heroic, realistic and historical – dwelling on the stirring rhetoric of battle, the documentary detail of war, the complexities of diplomacy and power; the Quarto staging the successful siege as a clever trick that happens to work. The Henry of the Quarto is presented not as an epic hero or an awe-inspiring historical character, but as a 'gentle gamester':

For when cruelty and lenitie play for a Kingdome,
The gentlest gamester is the sooner winner.

(p. 60)

Thus there are continual interrelations and transactions of meaning between 'serious' and 'comic' scenes, unpunctuated by any epic distancing. The dramatic structure of the Quarto allows for effects of great immediacy and dramatic dislocation: consider how a relaxed summit meeting in the French court gives sudden place to a scene of military violence:

King. Well for us, you shall returne our answer backe
To our brother England.

Exit omnes.

Enter Nim, Bardolfe, Pistoll, Boy.

Nim. Before God here is hote service.

(pp. 53–4)

One effect of this diminution of the principle of contrast by which 'high' and 'low' styles, epic and comedy, are juxtaposed is to draw

[26]

the figure of the king out of the remote distantiation of history and towards the everyday world of the popular audience. The cultural differentiation between king and commoners is thus reduced, and the play reconfigures a hierarchical society as a community united in the process of festival. This 'plebeianising' tendency of the Quartos has been noted:[20] but it is by no means the only effect of the play's investment in the comic-romance historical mode.

In *The Life of Henry the Fift* an epic style raises the discursive and ideological level of monarchy's representation to such a pitch that Henry's descent into the role of common man – as in the scene of his disguising before Agincourt – seems distastefully opportunistic and calculated. Yet that same epic style has the power to redeem Henry from any critical or interrogative implications released by that juxtaposition. The Folio's Chorus prepares the ground for Henry's conversation with the soldiers by its passionate celebration of 'The Royall Captaine of this Ruin'd Band', greeting all his soldiers as 'Brothers, Friends and Countreymen'. The king's quarrel with the soldier Williams raises a dangerous shadow of internal dissension: but one that is then redeemed, within the conventions of epic, by Henry's heart-searching soliloquy on the anxieties of kingship, and his heroic 'Crispin's Day' speech on the battlefield. In the Quarto text the debate with the soldiers is just as productive of critical questions as its counterpart in the Folio; and Williams's resistance to Henry's persuasions is actually intensified, since the words of acceptance – 'I would not have the king answere for me. / Yet I intend to fight lustily for him' – assigned in the Folio to Williams, is here attributed to another of the three soldiers. Henry's subsequent soliloquy ('O God of battels steele my souldiers harts', p. 67) is merely a prayer for forgiveness of his father's usurpation, and has nothing to declare about the relations between king and subject. Thus the penetrating questions posed by Williams continue to reverberate right into the battle itself; and Williams's final refusal to be humiliated by the royal jest carried all the pride and dignity of plebeian resistance to authority:

My Liege, all offences come from the heart:
Never came any from mine to offend your Majestie.
You appeard to me as a common man:
Witnesse the night, your garments, your lowlinesse,

Introduction

And whatsoever you received under that habit,
I beseech your Majestie impute it to youre owne fault
And not mine.

(p. 78)

The extraordinarily 'levelling' effect of this moment has much greater force in the Quarto than in the Folio text: since while in the latter the king consistently occupies the epic and historicist conventions appropriate to monarchy, occasionally stooping with studied calculation to the level of his subjects; in the Quarto a distinct plebeianising and carnivalisation of the monarch effectively sets Henry and Williams face to face, man to man, in a ritual enactment of that myth of equality that underlies the comic-romance motif of 'the king disguised'.[21] Williams's professional dignity and plebeian pride can be set against that orgiastic festival of violence, celebrated on the field of Agincourt, which in the Quarto aligns Henry very closely with Pistoll:

Alarum soundes

What new alarum is this?
Bid every souldier kill his prisoner.
  Pist. Couple gorge.   *Exit omnes.*

(p. 73)

★

The modest objective of this introduction is merely to open up the text to a new kind of inspection, uncontaminated by the prejudices of traditional scholarship. The purpose of this edition is to facilitate consideration of *The Cronicle History of Henry the fift* as a text valuable in its own right – a document of immeasurably more authority, as Gary Taylor admits, than any scholarly judgement or critical hypothesis – rather than as a text so deeply corrupt and inferior as to be virtually excluded from serious critical attention. After all, what does the bibliographical stigma of 'corruption' actually mean, other than the existence of some level of intervention into the processes of composition and transmission by hands other than that of the author? Since we have no means of knowing the extent to which authorial influence (as distinct from the influences of actors, theatre entrepreneurs, scribes, printers, pirates) uniquely

[28]

Introduction

determined the shape and content of the printed texts, we are stuck with a self-evidently and irredeemably collaborative cultural production. Why should this be a problem? Since it is generally agreed that the early modern drama was a highly collaborative cultural form, such collectively processed scripts would seem accurate and appropriate products of its collective methods.

In practice, however, this general acceptance of the 'Shakespearean' drama as a collective rather than an individual cultural form has not been permitted to dislodge the rigid hierarchy of functions implicitly assumed by traditional editorial practices: what the writer writes, others (actors, theatre entrepreneurs, scribes, printers, pirates) corrupt, mangle and pervert to illegitimate uses. The privileging and hypostatisation of the authorial function is of course a retrospective anachronism; the pervasive assumption of hierarchical precedence between the various functions (Shakespeare, for one, belonged to at least three of the categories listed here) is an entirely inappropriate model of the historical conditions of early modern culture. If 'corruption' then can be purged of its aura of moral transgression and translated as the collaborative, overdetermined productivity of the early modern theatre, in which the authentically Shakespearian input happily coexisted with a diversity of other influences, then texts like *The Cronicle History of Henry the fift* can at last hope to obtain a long-deserved currency. This edition now makes the play generally available, for the first time since the early seventeenth century, for the kind of practical experimentation and theoretical mobilisation which alone can genuinely test the validity of that scholarly consensus that has kept it now, for the best part of three centuries, virtually outside the scope of editorial reproduction, critical debate and theatrical performance.

NOTES AND REFERENCES

1. G.I. Duthie, 'The quarto of Shakespeare's *Henry V*', in *Papers Mainly Shakespearian* (Edinburgh: Oliver & Boyd, 1964) p. 117.
2. J.H. Walter (ed.), *King Henry V* (Arden Shakespeare) (London: Methuen, 1954), p. xxxviii.
3. *Ibid.*, p. xxxix.
4. Gary Taylor (ed.), *Henry V* (Oxford Shakespeare), (Oxford: Oxford University Press, 1984), p. 23.

5. *Ibid.*

6. *Ibid.*

7. *Ibid.*

8. Duthie (1964), p. 111.

9. *Ibid.*, p. 112.

10. Taylor (1984), p. 21.

11. *Ibid.*

12. Charlton Hinman (ed.), *The First Folio of Shakespeare* (Norton Facsimile) (London and New York: Paul Hamlyn, 1968), pp. 424–5.

13. Raphael Holinshed. *Chronicles of England, Scotlande and Irelande*, 2nd edition (London, 1577), vol. III, pp. 545–6.

14. Taylor (1984), p. 12.

15. Annabel Patterson, *Shakespeare and the Popular Voice* (Oxford: Blackwell, 1989); quoted from Graham Holderness (ed.), *Shakespeare's History Plays: 'Richard II' to 'Henry V'* (London: Macmillan, 1992), pp. 176–7.

16. *Ibid.*

17. See for example Graham Holderness, *Shakespeare: The Play of History* (London: Macmillan, 1987), pp. 62–84; and *Shakespeare Recycled* (Hemel Hempstead: Harvester Wheatsheaf, 1992), pp. 178–210.

18. Stephen Urkowitz, 'Good news about bad quartos', in Maurice Charney (ed.), *Bad Shakespeare: Revaluations of the Shakespeare Canon* (London and Toronto: Associated University Presses, 1988), p. 204.

19. *Ibid.*

20. Leah Marcus, 'Levelling Shakespeare: local customs and local texts', *Shakespeare Quarterly*, 42:ii (1991), pp. 168–78.

21. See Anne Barton, 'The king disguised: Shakespeare's *Henry V* and the comic history', in Joseph G. Price (ed.), *The Triple Bond* (University Park, PA: Pennsylvania State University Press, 1975).

Select Bibliography

Bate, Jonathan, 'Shakespeare's tragedies as working scripts', *Critical Survey*, 3:ii (1991), pp. 118–27.

Cloud, Random, [Randall McCleod], 'The marriage of good and bad quartos', *Shakespeare Quarterly*, 33:4 (1982), pp. 421–30.

Duthie, G.I., 'The quarto of Shakespeare's *Henry V*', in *Papers Mainly Shakespearian* (Edinburgh: Oliver & Boyd, 1964), pp. 106–30.

Grazia, Margareta de, 'The essential Shakespeare and the material book', *Textual Practice*, 2:i (1988), pp. 69–85.

Grazia, Margareta de, *Shakespeare Verbatim* (Oxford: Oxford University Press, 1991).

Hinman, Charlton, (ed.), *The First Folio of Shakespeare* (Norton Facsimile) (London and New York: Paul Hamlyn, 1968).

Holderness, Graham, Potter, Nick and Turner, John, *Shakespeare: the Play of History* (London: Macmillan, 1987).

Holderness, Graham, *Shakespeare Recycled* (Hemel Hempstead: Harvester Wheatsheaf, 1992).

Ioppolo, Grace, *Revising Shakespeare* (Cambridge, Mass.: Harvard University Press, 1991).

Marcus, Leah, 'Levelling Shakespeare: local customs and local texts', *Shakespeare Quarterly*, 42:ii (1991), pp. 168–78.

Orgel, Stephen, 'The authentic Shakespeare', *Representations* 21 (Winter 1988), pp. 1–26.

Parker, Brian, 'Bowers of bliss: deconflation in the Shakespeare canon', *New Theatre Quarterly*, 7:xxv (1991), pp. 357–61.

Patterson, Annabel, *Shakespeare and the Popular Voice* (Oxford: Blackwell, 1989).

Small, Ian and Walsh, Marcus (eds), *The Theory and Practice of Text-editing* (Cambridge: Cambridge University Press, 1991).

Taylor, Gary, (ed.), *Henry V* (Oxford Shakespeare) (Oxford: Oxford University Press, 1984).

Select Bibliography

Urkowitz, Stephen, 'Good news about bad quartos', in Maurice Charney (ed.), *Bad Shakespeare: Revaluations of the Shakespeare Canon* (London and Toronto: Associated University Presses, 1988).

Walter, J.H. (ed.), *King Henry V* (Arden Shakespeare) (London: Methuen, 1954).

Wells, Stanley, 'Theatricalizing Shakespeare's texts', *New Theatre Quarterly*, 7:xxvi (1991), pp. 184–6.

Textual History

T H I S play was initially published in 1600, in Quarto format, with the following title-page:

THE
CRONICLE

History of Henry the fift,
With his battell fought at *Agin Court* in
France.   Togither with *Auntient
Pistoll.*

*As it hath bene sundry times playd by the Right honorable
the Lord Chamberlaine his servants.*

L O N D O N

Printed by *Thomas Creede*, for Tho. Milling-
ton, and Iohn Busby. And are to be
sold at his house in Carter lane, next
the Powle head.   1600.

An original copy is held in the British Library. Second and third editions of this Quarto were printed by Thomas Creede for Thomas Pavier in 1602 and 1608. The second is a straightforward reprint; the third, printed from the first, added some words and redivided some lines. A facsimile was published for the New Shakespeare Society in 1875: *The Chronicle History of Henry the*

[33]

Fifth: reprint of First Quarto, 1600, introduction by B. Nicholson (London: N. Trubner and Co., Ltd., 1975). A modern version of the text appears in *Shakespeare's Plays in Quarto*, eds. Michael Allen and Kenneth Muir (Berkeley and Los Angeles, 1981).

THE

CRONICLE

Hiſtory of Henry the fift,

With his battell fought at *Agin Court* in
France. Togither with *Auntient
Piſtoll.*

*As it hath bene ſundry times playd by the Right honorable
the Lord Chamberlaine his ſeruants.*

LONDON

Printed by *Thomas Creede*, for Tho. Milling-
ton, and Iohn Busby   And are to be
ſold at his houſe in Carter Lane, next
the Powle head.   1600.

Henry the fift,

With his battell fought at
Agin Court in *France*.
Togither with *Auntient Pistoll*.

Enter King Henry, Exeter, 2. *Bishops*, Clarence, *and other Attendants*.

Exeter.

Shall I call in Thambassadors my Liege?
   King. Not yet my Cousin, til we be resolvde
Of some serious matters touching us and *France*.
   Bi. God and his Angels guard your sacred throne,
And make you long become it.
   King. Shure we thank you. And good my Lord proceed
Why the Lawe *Salicke* which they have in *France*,
Or should or should not, stop us in our clayme :
And God forbid my wise and learned Lord,
That you should fashion, frame, or wrest the same.
For God doth know how many now in health,
Shall drop their blood in approbation,
Of what your reverence shall incite us too.
Therefore take heed how you impawne our person,
How you awake the sleeping sword of warre :
We charge you in the name of God take heed.
After this conjuration, speake my Lord :
And we will judge, note, and beleeve in heart,
That what you speake, is washt as pure
As sin in baptisme.

[*Bish.*] Then heare me gracious soveraigne, and you peeres,
Which owe your lives, your faith and services
To this imperiall throne.
There is no bar to stay your highnesse claime to *France*
But one, which they produce from *Faramount*,
No female shall succeed in salicke land,
Which salicke land the French unjustly gloze
To be the realme of *France* :
And *Faramont* the founder of this law and female barre :
Yet their owne writers faithfully affirme
That the land salicke lyes in *Germany*,
Betweene the flouds of *Sabeck* and of *Elme*,
Where *Charles* the fift having subdude the Saxons,
There left behind, and setled certaine French,
Who holding in disdaine the Germaine women,
For some dishonest maners of their lives,
Establisht there this lawe. To wit,
No female shall succeed in salicke land :
Which salicke land as I said before,
Is at this time in *Germany* called *Mesene* :
Thus doth it well appeare the salicke lawe
Was not devised for the realme of *France*,
Nor did the French possesse the salicke land,
Untill 400. one and twentie yeares
After the function of king *Faramont*,
Godly supposed the founder of this lawe :
Hugh Capet also that usurpt the crowne,
To fine his title with some showe of truth,
When in pure truth it was corrupt and naught :
Convaid himselfe as heire to the Lady *Inger*,
Daughter to *Charles*, the foresaid Duke of *Lorain*,
So that as cleare as is the sommers Sun,
King *Pippins* title and *Hugh Capets* claime,
King *Charles* his satisfaction all appeare,
To hold in right and title of the female :
So do the Lords of *France* until this day,
Howbeit they would hold up this salick lawe

To bar your highnesse claiming from the female,
And rather choose to hide them in a net,
Then amply to imbace their crooked causes,
Usurpt from you and your progenitors.   (claime?
   K. May we with right & conscience make this
   Bi. The sin upon my head dread soveraigne.
For in the booke of Numbers is it writ,
When the sonne dies, let the inheritance
Descend unto the daughter.
Noble Lord stand for your owne,
Unwinde your bloody flagge,
Go my dread Lord to your great graunsirs grave,
From whom you clayme :
And your great Uncle *Edward* the blacke Prince,
Who on the French ground playd a Tragedy
Making defeat on the full power of *France*,
Whilest his most mighty father on a hill,
Stood smiling to behold his Lyons whelpe,
Foraging blood of French Nobilitie.
O Noble English that could entertaine
With halfe their Forces the full power of *France* :
And let an other halfe stand laughing by,
All out of worke, and cold for action.
   King. We must not onely arme us against the French,
But lay downe our proportion for the Scot,
Who will make rode upon us with all advantages.
   Bi. The Marches gracious soveraigne, shalbe sufficient
To guardyour *England* from the pilfering borderers.
   King. We do not meane the coursing sneakers onely,
But feare the mayne entendement of the Scot,
For you shall read, never my great grandfather
Unmaskt his power for *France*,
But that the Scot on his unfurnisht Kingdome,
Came pouring like the Tide into a breach,
That *England* being empty of defences,
Hath shooke and trembled at the brute hereof.
   Bi. She hath bin then more feared then hurt my Lord :

For heare her but examplified by her selfe,
When all her chivalry hath bene in *France*
And she a mourning widow of her Nobles,
She hath her selfe not only well defended,
But taken and impounded as a stray, the king of Scots,
Whom like a caytiffe she did leade to *France*,
Filling your Chronicles as rich with praise
As is the owse and bottome of the sea
With sunken wrack and shiplesse treasurie.

   Lord. There is a saying very old and true,
If you will *France* win,
Then with *Scotland* first begin:
For once the Eagle, England being in pray,
To his unfurnish nest the weazel Scot
Would suck her egs, playing the mouse in absence of the
To spoyle and havock more then she can eat.   (cat :

   Exe. It followes then, the cat must stay at home,
Yet that is but a curst necessitie,
Since we have trappes to catch the petty theeves :
Whilste that the armed hand doth fight abroad
The advised head controlles at home :
For government though high and lowe, being put into parts,
Congrueth with a mutual consent like musicke.

   Bi. True : therefore doth heaven divide the fate of man
         in divers functions.
Whereto is added as an ayme or but, obedience :
For so live the honey Bees, creatures that by awe
Ordaine an act of order to a peopeld Kingdome :
They have a King and officers of sort,
Where some like Magistrates correct at home :
Others like Marchants venture trade abroad :
Others like souldiers armed in their stings,
Make boote upon the sommers velvet bud :
Which pillage they with mery march bring home
To the tent royall of their Emperour,
Who busied in his majestie, behold
The singing masons building roofes of gold :

[40]

The civell citizens lading up the honey,
The said eyde Justice with his surly humme,
Delivering up to executors pale, the lazy caning Drone.
This I infer, that 20. actions once a foote,
May all end in one moment.
As many Arrowes losed severall wayes, flye to one marke :
As many severall wayes meete in one towne :
As many fresh streames run in one selfe sea :
As many lines close in the dyall center :
So may a thousand actions once a foote,
End in one moment, and be all well borne without defect.
Therefore my Liege to *France*,
Divide your happy England into foure,
Of which take you one quarter into *France*,
And you withall, shall make all *Gallia* shake.
If we with thrice that power left at home,
Cannot defend our owne doore from the dogge,
Let us be beaten, and from henceforth lose
The name of pollicy and hardinesse.
   Ki. Call in the messenger sent from the Dolphin.
And by your ayde, the noble sinewes of our land,
France being ours, weele bring it to our awe,
Or breake it all in peeces :
Eyther our Chronicles shal with full mouth speak
Freely of our acts,
Or else like toonglesse mutes
Not worshipt with a paper Epitaph :

Enter Thambassadors from France.

Now are we well prepared to know the Dolphins pleasure,
For we heare your comming is from him.
   Ambassa. Pleaseth your Majestie to give us leav
Freely to render what we have in charge :
Or shall I sparingly shew a farre off,
The Dolphins pleasure and our Embassage?
   King. We are no tyrant, but a Christian King,
To whom our spirit is as subject,

[41]

As are our wretches fettered in our prisons.
Therefore freely and with uncurbed boldnesse
Tell us the Dolphins minde.

    Ambas. Then this in fine the Dolphin saith,
Whereas you clayme certaine Townes in *France*,
From your predecessor king *Edward* the third,
This he returnes.

He saith, theres nought in *France* that can be with a nimble
Galliard wonne : you cannot revel into Dukedomes there :
Therefore he sendeth meeter for your study,
This tunne of treasure : and in lieu of this,
Desires to let the Dukedomes that you crave
Heare no more from you : This the Dolphin saith.

    King. What treasure Uncle?

    Exe. Tennis balles my Liege.

    King. We are glad the Dolphin is so pleasant with us,
Your message and his present we accept :
When we have matched our rackets to these balles,
We will by Gods grace play such a set,
Shall strike his fathers crowne into the hazard.
Tell him he hath made a match with such a wrangler,
That all the Courts of *France* shall be disturbd with chases.
And we understand him well, how he comes ore us
With our wilder dayes, not measuring what use we made
        of them.
We never valued this poore seate of England.
And therefore gave our selves to barbarous licence :
As tis common seene that men are merriest when they are
        from home.
But tell the Dolphin we will keepe our state,
Be like a King, mightie and commaund,
When we do rowse us in throne of *France* :
For this have we laid by our Majestie
And plodded lide a man for working dayes.
But we will rise there with so full of glory,
That we will dazel all the eyes of *France*,
I strike the Dolphin blinde to looke on us,

And tell him this, his mock hath turnd his balles to gun
　　　　　　　　　　　　　　　　(stones,
And his soule shall sit sore charged for the wastfull
　　　　　　　　　　　　　　　(vengeance
That shall flye from them. For this his mocke
Shall mocke many a wife out of their deare husbands.
Mocke mothers from their sonnes, mocke Castles downe,
I some are yet ungotten and unborne,
That shall have cause to curse the Dolphins scorne.
But this lyes all within the will of God, to whom we doo
　　　　　　　　　　　　　　　　(appeale,
And in whose name tel you the Dolphin we are comming on
To venge us as we may, and to put forth our hand
In a rightfull cause : so get you hence, and tell your Prince,
His Jest will savour but of shallow wit,
When thousands weepe, more then did laugh at it.
Convey them with safe conduct : see them hence.
　　Exe. This was a merry message.
　　King. We hope to make the sender blush at it :
Therfore let our collection for the wars be soone provided :
For God before, weell check the Dolphin at his fathers
　　　　　　　　　　　　　　　　(doore.
Therefore let every man now taske his thought,
That this faire action may on foote be brought.

　　　　　　　　　　　　　　　　Exeunt omnes.

　　　　　　Enter Nim *and* Bardolfe.

　　Bar. Godmorrow Corporall *Nim.*
　　Nim. Godmorrow Lieftenant *Bardolfe.*
　　Bar. What is antient *Pistoll* and thee friends yet?
　　Nim. I cannot tell, things must be as they may :
I dare not fight, but I will winke and hold out mine Iron :
It is a simple one, but what tho ; it will serve to toste cheese.
And it will endure cold as an other mans sword will,
And theres the humor of it.

[43]

Bar. Yfaith mistresse quickly did thee great wrong,
For thou weart troth plight to her.

Nim. I must do as I may, tho patience be a tyred mare,
Yet sheel plod, and some say knives have edges,
And men may sleepe and have their throtes about them
At that time, and there is the humour of it.

Bar. Come y faith, Ile bestow a breakfast to make *Pistoll*
And thee friendes. What a plague should we carrie knives
To cut our owne throates.

Nim. Y faith Ile live as long as I may, thats the certaine of it.
And when I cannot live any longer, Ile do as I may,
And theres my rest, and the randevous of it.

Enter Pistoll *and Hostes Quickly, his wife.*

Bar. Godmorrow ancient *Pistoll*.
Here comes ancient *Pistoll*, I prithee *Nim* be quiet.

Nim. How do you my Hoste?

Pist. Base slave, callest thou me hoste?
Now by gads lugges I sweare, I scorne the title,
Nor shall my *Nell* keepe lodging.

Host. No by my troath not I,
For we cannot bed nor boord half a score honest gentlwomen
That live honestly by the price of their needle,
But it is thought straight we keepe a bawdy-house.
O Lord heeres Corporall *Nims*, now shall
We have wilful adultry and murther committed :
Good Corporall *Nim* shew the valour of a man,
And put up your sword.

Nim. Push.

Pist. What dost thou push, thou prickeard cur of Iseland?

Nim. Will you shog off? I would have you solus.

Pist. Solus egregious dog, that solus in thy throte,
And in thy lungs, and which is worse, within
Thy mesfull mouth, I do retort that solus in thy
Bowels, and in thy Jaw, perdie : for I can talke,
And *Pistolls* flashing firy cock is up.

Nim. I am not *Barbasom*, you cannot conjure me :

[44]

Henry the fift

I have an humour *Pistoll* to knock you indifferently well,
And you fall foule with me *Pistoll*, Ile scoure you with my
Rapier in faire termes. If you will walke off a little,
Ile prick your guts a litle in good termes,
And theres the humour of it.

    Pist. O braggard vile, and damned furious wight,
The Grave doth gape, and groaning
Death is neare, therefore exall.

                        They drawe.

    Bar. Heare me, he that strikes the first blow,
Ile kill him, as I am a souldier.

    Pist. An oath of mickle might, and fury shall abate.

    Nim. Ile cut your throat at one time or an other in faire
And theres the humour of it.   (termes,

    Pist. Couple gorge is the word, I thee defie agen :
A damned hound, thinkst thou my spouse to get?
No, to the powdering tub of infamy,
Fetch forth the lazar kite of Cresides kinde
Doll Tear-sheete, she by name, and her espowse,
I have, and I will hold, the quandom quickly,
For the onely she and Paco, there it is inough.

                 Enter the Boy.

    Boy. Hostes you must come straight to my maister,
And you Host *Pistoll.* Good *Bardolfe*
Put thy nose betweene the sheetes, and do the office of a
                                  (warming pan.

    Host. By my troath heele yeeld the crow a pudding one
                                  (of these dayes.
Ile go to him, husband youle come?

    Bar. Come *Pistoll* be friends.
Nim prithee be friends, and if thou wilt not be
Enemies with me too.

    Ni. I shal have my eight shillings I woon of you at beating?

    Pist. Base is the slave that payes.

    Nim. That now I will have, and theres the humor of it.

Pist. As manhood shall compound.   *They draw.*

Bar. He that strikes the first blow,

Ile kill him by this sword.

  Pist. Sword is an oath, and oathes must have their course.

  Nim. I shall have my eight shillings I wonne of you at
        beating?

  Pist. A noble shalt thou have, and readie pay,

And liquor likewise will I give to thee,

And friendship shall combind and brotherhood :

Ile live by *Nim* as *Nim* shall live by me :

Is not this just? for I shall Sutler be

Unto the Campe, and profit will occrue.

  Nim. I shall have my noble?

  Pist. In cash most truly paid.

  Nim. Why theres the humour of it.

Enter Hostes.

  Hostes. As ever you came of men come in,

Sir *John* poore soule is so troubled

With a burning tashan contigian fever, tis wonderfull.

  Pist. Let us condoll the knight : for lamkins we will live.

                        Exeunt omnes

Enter Exeter and Gloster.

  Glost. Before God my Lord, his Grace is too bold to trust
        these traytors.

  Exe. They shalbe apprehended by and by.

  Glost. I but the man that was his bedfellow

Whom he hath cloyed and graced with princely favours

That he should for a forraine purse, to sell

His Soveraignes life to death and trechery.

  Exe. O the Lord of *Massham.*

Enter the King and three Lords.

  King. Now sirs the windes faire, and we wil aboord ;

My Lord of *Cambridge*, and my Lord of *Massham*,

Henry the fift

And you my gentle Knight, give me your thoughts,
Do you not thinke the power we beare with us,
Will make us conquerors in the field of *France*?

   Masha. No doubt my Liege, if each man do his best.

   Cam. Never was Monarch better feared and loved then
      is your majestie.

   Gray. Even those that were your fathers enemies
Have steeped their galles in honey for your sake.

   King. We therefore have great cause of thankfulnesse,
And shall forget the office of our hands :
Sooner then reward and merit,
According to their cause and worthinesse.

   Masha. So service shall with steeled sinewes shine,
And labour shall refresh it selfe with hope
To do your Grace incessant service.

   King. Uncle of *Exeter*, enlarge the man
Committed yesterday, that rayled against our person,
We consider it was the heate of wine that set him on,
And on his more advice we pardon him.

   Masha. That is mercie but too much securitie :
Let him bee punisht Soveraigne, least the example of
Breed more of such a kinde.   (him,

   King. O let us yet be mercifull.

   Cam. So may your highnesse, and punish too.

   Gray. You shew great mercie if you give him life,
After the taste of his correction.

   King. Alas your too much care and love of me
Are heavy orisons gainst the poore wretch,
If litle faults proceeding on distemper should not bee
                     (winked at,
How should we stretch our eye, when capitall crimes,
Chewed, swallowed and disgested, appeare before us :
Well yet enlarge the man, tho Cambridge and the rest
In their deare loves, and tender preservation of our state,
Would have him punisht.
Now to our French causes.
Who are the late Commissioners?

Cam. Me one my Lord, your highnesse bad me aske for
    it to day.
Mash. So did you me my Soveraigne.
Gray. And me my Lord.
King. Then *Richard* Earle of *Cambridge* there is yours.
There is yours my Lord of *Masham*.
And sir *Thomas Gray* knight of *Northumberland*, this same is
Read them, and know we know your worthinesse. (yours :
Unckle *Exeter* I will aboord to night.
Why how now Gentlemen, why change you colour?
What see you in those papers
That hath so chased your blood out of apparance?
    Cam. I do confesse my fault, and do submit me
To your highnesse mercie.
    Mash. To which we all appeale.
    King. The mercy which was quit in us but late,
By your owne reasons is forestald and done :
You must not dare for shame to aske for mercy,
For your owne conscience turne upon your bosomes,
As dogs upon their maisters worrying them.
See you my Princes, and my noble Peeres,
These English monsters :
My Lord of *Cambridge* here,
You know how apt we were to grace him,
In all things belonging to his honour :
And this vilde man hath for a fewe light crownes,
Lightly conspired and sworne unto the practises of *France* :
To kill us here in *Hampton*. To the which,
This knight no lesse in bountie bound to us
Then *Cambridge* is, haah likewise sworne.
But oh what shall I say to thee false man,
Thou cruell ingratefull and inhumane creature,
Thou that didst beare the key of all my counsell,
That knewst the very secrets of my heart,
That almost mightest a coyned me into gold,
Wouldest thou a practisde on me for thy use :
Can it be possible that out of thee

Should proceed one sparke that might annoy my finger?
Tis so strange, that tho the truth doth showe as grose
As black from white, mine eye wil scarcely see it.
Their faults are open, arrest them to the answer of the lawe,
And God acquit them of their practises.

   Exe. I arrest thee of high treason,
By the name of *Richard*, Earle of *Cambridge.*
I arest thee of high treason,
By the name of *Henry*, Lord of *Masham.*
I arest thee of high treason,
By the name of *Thomas Gray*, knight of *Northumberland.*

   Mash. Our purposes God justly hath discovered,
And I repent my fault more then my death,
Which I beseech your majestie forgive,
Altho my body pay the price of it.

   King. God quit you in his mercy. Heare your sentence.
You have conspired against our royall person,
Joyned with an enemy proclaimed and fixed.
And from his coffers received the golden earnest of our death
Touching our person we seeke no redresse.
But we our kingdomes safetie must so tender
Whose ruine you have sought,
That to our lawes we do deliver you.   death,
Get ye therefore hence : poore miserable creatures to your
The taste whereof, God in his mercy give you   (amisse :
Patience to endure, and true repentance of all your deeds
Beare them hence.

                               Exit three Lords.

Now Lords to *France.* The enterprise whereof,
Shall be to you as us, successively.
Since God cut off this dangerous treason lurking in our way
Cheerly to sea, the signes of war advance :
No King of England, if not King of *France.*

                    Exit omnes.

Enter Nim, Pistoll, Bardolfe, Hostes and a Boy.

Host. I prethy sweete heart, let me bring thee so farre as
(*Stanes,*

Pist. No fur, no fur.

Bar. Well sir *John* is gone. God be with him.

Host. I, he is in *Arthors* bosom, if ever any were :
He went away as if it were a crysombd childe,
Betweene twelve and one,
Just at turning of the tide :
His nose was as sharpe as a pen :
For when I saw him fumble with the sheetes,
And talk of floures, and smile upon his fingers ends
I knew there was no way but one.
How now sir *John* quoth I?
And he cryed three times, God, God, God,
Now I to comfort him, bad him not think of God,
I hope there was no such need.
Then he bad me put more cloathes at his feete :
And I felt to them, and they were as cold as any stone :
And to his knees, and they were as cold as any stone.
And so upward, and upward, and all was as cold as any stone.

Nim. They say he cride out on Sack.

Host. I that he did.

Boy. And of women.

Host. No that he did not.

Boy. Yet that he did : and he sed they were divels incarnat.

Host. Indeed carnation was a colour he never loved.

Nim. Well he did cry out on women.

Host. Indeed he did in some sort handle women,
But then he was rumaticke, and talkt of the whore of
(*Babylon.*

Boy. Hostes do you remember he saw a Flea stand
Upon *Bardolfes* Nose, and sed it was a black soule
Burning in hell fire?

Bar. Well, God be with him,
That was all the wealth I got in his service.

Nim. Shall we shog off?
The king wil be gone from *Southampton.*
   Pist. Cleare up thy cristalles,
Looke to my chattels and my moveables.
Trust none : the word is pitch and pay :
Mens words are wafer cakes,
And holdfast is the only dog my deare.
Therefore cophetua be thy counsellor,
Touch her soft lips and part.
   Bar. Farewell hostes.
   Nim. I cannot kis : and theres the humor of it.
But adieu
   Pist. Keepe fast thy buggle boe.

                            Exit omnes.

        Enter King of France, Bourbon, Dolphin,
               and others.

   King. Now you Lords of *Orleance,*
Of *Bourbon,* and of *Berry,*
You see the King of England is not slack,
For he is footed on this land alreadie.
   Dolphin. My gratious Lord, tis meet we all goe
And arme us against the foe :   (foorth,
And view the weak & sickly parts of *France* :
But let us do it with no show of feare,
No with no more, then if we heard
England were busied with a Moris dance.
For my good Lord, she is so idely kingd,
Her scepter so fantastically borne,
So guided by a shallow humorous youth,
That feare attends her not.
   Con. O peace Prince *Dolphin,* you deceive your selfe,
Question your grace the late Embassador,
With what regard he heard his Embassage,
How well supplied with aged Counsellours,

And how his resolution andswered him,
You then would say that *Harry* was not wilde.
   King. Well thinke we *Harry* strong :
And strongly arme us to prevent the foe.
   Con. My Lord here is an Embassador
From the King of England.
   King. Bid him come in.
You see this chase is hotly followed Lords.
   Dol. My gracious father, cut up this English short,
Selfelove my Liege is not so vile a thing,
As selfe neglecting.

Enter Exeter

   King. From our brother England?
   Exe. From him, and thus he greets your Majestie :
He wils you in the name of God Almightie,
That you devest your selfe and lay apart
That borrowed tytle, which by gift of heaven,
Of lawe of nature, and of nations, longs
To him and to his heires, namely the crowne
And all wide stretched titles that belongs
Unto the Crowne of *France*, that you may know
Tis no sinister, nor no awkeward claime,
Pickt from the worm holes of old vanisht dayes,
Nor from the dust of old oblivion rackte,
He sends you these most memorable lynes,
In every branch truly demonstrated :
Willing you overlooke this pedrigree,
And when you finde him evenly derived
From his most famed and famous ancestors,
Edward the third, he bids you then resigne
Your crowne and kingdome, indirectly held
From him, the native and true challenger.
   King. If not, what followes?
   Exe. Bloody constraint, for if you hide the crown
Even in your hearts, there will he rake for it :
Therefore in fierce tempest is he comming,

[52]

In thunder, and in earthquake, like a *Jove*,
That if requiring faile, he will compell it :
And on your heads turnes he the widowes teares,
The Orphanes cries, the dead mens bones,
The pining maydens grones.
For husbands, fathers, and distressed lovers,
Which shall be swallowed in this controversie.
This is his claime, his threatning, and my message.
Unles the *Dolphin* be in presence here,
To whom expresly we bring greeting too.

Dol. For the *Dolphin*? I stand here for him,
What to heare from England.

Exe. Scorn & defiance, slight regard, contempt,
And any thing that may not misbecome
The mightie sender, doth he prise you at :
Thus saith my king. Unles your fathers highnesse
Sweeten the bitter mocke you sent his Majestie,
Heele call you to so loud an answere for it,
That caves and wombely vaultes of *France*
Shall chide your trespasse, and return your mock,
In second accent of his ordenance.

Dol. Say that my father render faire reply,
It is against my will :
For I desire nothing so much,
As oddes with England.
And for that cause according to his youth
I did present him with those *Paris* balles.

Exe. Heele make your *Paris* Lover shake for it,
Were it the mistresse Court of mightie *Europe*.
And be assured, youle finde a difference
As we his subjects have in wonder found :
Betweene his yonger dayes and these he musters now,
Now he wayes time even to the latest graine,
Which you shall finde in your owne losses
If he stay in *France*.

King. Well for us, you shall returne our answere backe
To our brother England.

[53]

Exit omnes.

Enter Nim, Bardolfe, Pistoll, Boy.

Nim. Before God here is hote service.

Pist. Tis hot indeed, blowes go and come,
Gods vassals drop and die.

Nim. Tis honor, and theres the humor of it.

Boy. Would I were in London :
Ide given all my honor for a pot of Ale.

Pist. And I. If wishes would prevaile,
I would not stay, but thither would I hie.

Enter Flewellen *and beates them in.*

Flew. Godes plud up to the breaches
You rascals, will you not up to the breaches?

Nim. Abate thy rage sweete knight,
Abate thy rage.

Boy. Well I would I were once from them :
They would have me as familiar
With mens pockets, as their gloves, and their
Handkerchers, they will steale anything.
Bardolfe stole a Lute case, carryed it three mile,
And sold it for three hapence.
Nim stole a fier shovell.
I knew by that, they meant to carry coales :
Well, if they will not leave me,
I meane to leave them.

Exit Nim, Bardolfe, Pistoll, *and the Boy.*

Enter Gower.

Gower. Gaptain *Flewellen*, you must come strait
To the Mines, to the Duke of *Gloster.*

Fleu. Looke you, tell the Duke it is not so good
To come to the mines : the concuaveties is otherwise.
You may discusse to the Duke, the enemy is digd
Himselfe five yardes under the countermines :

Henry the fift

By *Jesus* I thinke heele blowe up all
If there be no better direction.

Enter the King and his Lords alarum.

King. How yet resolves the Governour of the Towne?
This is the latest parley weele admit :
Therefore to our best mercie give your selves,
Or like to men proud of destruction, defie us to our worst,
For as I am a souldier, a name that in my thoughts
Becomes me best, if we begin the battery once againe
I will not leave the halfe atchieved Harflew,
Till in her ashes she be buried,
The gates of mercie are all shut up.
What say you, will you yeeld and this avoyd,
Or guiltie in defence be thus destroyd?

Enter Governour.

Gover. Our expectation hath this day end :
The Dolphin whom of succour we entreated,
Returnes us word, his powers are not yet ready,
To raise so great a siege : therefore dread King,
We yeeld our towne and lives to thy soft mercie :
Enter our gates, dispose of us and ours,
For we no longer are defensive now.

Enter Katherine, Allice.

Kate. Alice venecia, vous aves cates en,
Vou parte fort bon Angloys englatara,
Coman sae palla vou la main en francoy.
  Allice. La main madam de han.
  Kate. E da bras.
  Allice. De arma madam.
  Kate. Le main da han la bras de arma.
  Allice. Owy e madam.
  Kate. E Coman sa pella vow la menton a la coll.
  Allice. De neck, e de cin, madam,

[55]

Kate. E de neck, e de cin, e de code.

Allice. De cudie may foy Je oblye, mais Je remembre,
Le tude, o de elbo madam.

Kate. Ecowte Je rehersera, towt cella que Jac apoandre,
De han, de arma, de neck, du cin, e de bilbo.

Allice. De elbo madam.

Kate. O Jesu, Jea obloye ma foy, ecoute Je recontera
De han, de arma, de neck, de cin, e de elbo, e ca bon.

Allice. Ma foy madam, vow parla au se bon Angloys
Asie vous aves ettue en Englatara.

Kate. Par la grace de deu an pettie tanes, Je parle milleur
Coman se pella vou le peid e le robe.

Allice. Le foot, e le con.

Kate. Le fot, e le con, ô Jesu! Je ne vew poinct parle,
Sie plus devant le che chevalires de franca,
Pur one million ma foy.

Allice, Madam, de foote, e le con.

Kate. O et ill ausie, ecowte Allice, de han, de arma,
De neck, de cin, le foote, e de con.

Allice. Cet fort bon madam.

Kate. Aloues a diner.

Exit omnes.

Enter King of France *Lord Constable, the Dolphin,
and* Burbon.

King. Tis certaine he is past the River Some.

Con. Mordeu ma via : Shall a few spranes of us,
The emptying of our fathers luxerie,
Outgrow their grafters.

Bur. Normanes, basterd Normanes, mor du
And if they passe unfoughtwithall,
Ile sell my Dukedome for a foggy farme
In that short nooke Ile of England.

Const. Why whence have they this mettall?
Is not their clymate raw, foggy and colde.
On whom as in disdaine, the Sunne lookes pale?

Can barley broath, a drench for swolne Jades
Their sodden water decockt such lively blood?
And shall our quick blood spirited with wine
Seeme frosty? O for honour of our names,
Let us not hang like frozen Iicesickles
Upon our houses tops, while they a more frosty clymate
Sweate drops of youthfull blood.

   King. Constable dispatch, send Montjoy forth,
To know what willing raunsome he will give?
Sonne *Dolphin* you shall stay in *Rone* with me.

   Dol. Not so I do beseech your Majestie.

   King. Well, I say it shalbe so.

Exeunt omnes.

Enter Gower.

   Go. How now Captain *Flewellen*, come you from the bridge?

   Flew. By Jesus thers excellent service committed at ye bridge.

   Gour. Is the Duke of *Exeter* safe?

   Flew. The duke of *Exeter* is a man whom I love, & I honor,
And I worship, with my soule, and my heart, and my life,
And my lands and my livings,
And my uttermost powers.
The Duke is looke you,
God be praised and pleased for it, no harme in the worell.
He is maintain the bridge very gallently : there is an Ensigne
There, I do not know how you call him, but by Jesus I think
He is as valient a man as *Marke Anthonie*, he doth maintain
the bridge most gallantly : yet he is a man of no reckoning :
But I did see him do gallant service.

   Gouer. How do you call him?

   Flew. His name is ancient *Pistoll.*

   Gouer. I know him not.

Enter Ancient Pistoll.

[57]

Flew. Do you not know him, here comes the man.

Pist. Captaine, I thee beseech to do me favour,
The Duke of *Exeter* doth love thee well.

Flew. I, and I praise God I have merrited some love at
(his hands.

Pist. *Bardolfe* a souldier, one of buxsome valour,
Hath by furious fate
And giddy Fortunes fickel wheele,
That Godes blinde that stands upon the rowling restlesse
(stone.

Flew. By your patience ancient *Pistoll*,
Fortune, looke you is painted,
Plind with a mufler before her eyes,
To signifie to you, that Fortune is plind :
And she is moreover painted with a wheele,
Which is the morall that Fortune is turning,
And inconstant, and variation ; and mutabilities :
And her fate is fixed at a sphericall stone
Which roules, and roules, and roules :
Surely the Poet is make an excellent description of Fortune.
Fortune looke you is and excellent morall.

Pist. Fortune is *Bardolfes* foe, and frownes on him,
For he hath stolne a packs, and hanged must he be :
A damned death, let gallowes gape for dogs,
Let man go free, and let not death his windpipe stop.
But *Exeter* hath given the doome of death,
For packs of pettie price :
Therefore go speake, the Duke will heare thy voyce,
And let not *Bardolfes* vitall threed be cut,
With edge of penny cord, and vile approach.
Speake Captaine for his life, and I will thee requite.

Flew. Captain *Pistoll*, I partly understand your meaning.

Pist. Why then rejoyce therefore.

Flew. Certainly Ancient *Pistol*, tis not a thing to rejoyce at,
For if he were my owne brother, I would wish the Duke
To do his pleasure, and put him to executions : for look you,
Disciplines ought to be kept, they ought to be kept.

[58]

Pist. Die and be damned, and figa for thy friendship,
Flew. That is good.
Pist. The figge of *Spaine* within thy Jawe.
Flew. That is very well.
Pist. I say the fig within thy bowels and thy durty maw.

Exit Pistoll.

Fle. Captain *Gour*, cannot you hear it lighten & thunder?
Gour. Why is this the Ancient you told me of?
I remember him now, he is a bawd, a cutpurse.
Flew. By Jesus heeis utter as prave words upon the bridge
As you shall desire to see in a sommers day, but its all one,
What he had sed to me, looke you, is all one.
Go. Why this is a gull, a foole, a rogue that goes to the wars
Onely to grace himselfe at his returne to London :
And such fellowes as he,
Are perfect in great Commaunders names.
They will learne by rote where services were done,
At such and such a sconce, at such a breach,
At such a convoy : who came off bravely, who was shot,
Who disgraced, what termes the enemie stood on.
And this they con perfectly in phrase of warre,
Which they trick up with new tuned oathes, & what a berd
Of the Generalls cut, and a horid shout of the campe
Will do among the foming bottles and alewasht wits
Is wonderfull to be thought on : but you must learne
To know such slaunders of this age,
Or else you may marvellously be mistooke,
Flew. Certain captain *Gower*, it is not the man, looke you,
That I did take him to be : but when time shall serve,
I shall tell him a litle of my desires : here comes his Majestie.

Enter King, Clarence, Gloster *and others.*

King. How now *Flewellen*, come you from the bridge?
Flew. I and it shall please your Majestie,
There is excellent service at the bridge.
King. What men have you lost *Flewellen?*

[59]

Flew. And it shall please your Majestie,
The partition of the adversarie hath bene great,
Very reasonably great : but for our own parts, like you now,
I thinke we have lost never a man, unlesse it be one
For robbing of a church, one *Bardolfe*, if your Majestie
Know the man, his face is full of whelkes and knubs,
And pumples, and his breath blowes at his nose
Like a cole, sometimes red, sometimes plew :
But god be praised, now his nose is executed, & his fire out.
 King. We would have all offenders so cut off,
And we here give expresse commaundment,
That there be nothing taken from the villages but paid for,
None of the French abused,
Or abraided with disdainfull language :
For when cruelty and lenitie play for a Kingdome,
The gentlest gamester is the sooner winner.

Enter French Herauld.

 Hera. You know me by my habit.
 Ki. Well then, we know thee, what shuld we know of thee?
 Hera. My maisters minde.
 King. Unfold it.
 Heral. Go thee unto *Harry of England*, and tell him,
Advantage is a better souldier then rashnesse :
Altho we did seeme dead, we did but slumber.
Now we speake upon our kue, and our voyce is imperiall,
England shall repent her folly: see her rashnesse,
And admire our sufferance. Which to raunsome,
His pettinesse would bow under :
For the effusion of our blood, his army is too weake :
For the disgrace we have borne, himselfe
Kneeling at our feete, a weake and worthlesse satisfaction.
To this, adde defyance. So much from the king my maister.
 King. What is thy name? we know thy qualitie.
 Herald. Montjoy.
 King. Thou dost thy office faire, returne thee backe,
And tell thy King, I do not seeke him now :

[60]

But could be well content, without impeach,
To march on to *Callis* : for to say the sooth,
Though tis no wisdome to confesse so much
Unto an enemie of craft and vantage.
My souldiers are with sicknesse much infeebled,
My Army lessoned, and those fewe I have,
Almost no better then so many French :
Who when they were in heart, I tell thee Herauld,
I thought upon one paire of English legges,
Did march three French mens.
Yet forgive me God, that I do brag thus :
This your heire of *France* hath blowne this vice in me.
I must repent, go tell thy maister here I am,
My raunsome is this frayle and worthlesse body,
My Army but a weake and sickly guarde.
Yet God before, we will come on,
If *France* and such an other neighbour stood in our way :
If we may passe, we will : if we be hindered,
We shall your tawny ground with your red blood discolour.
So *Montjoy* get you gone, there is for your paines :
The sum of all our answere is but this,
We would not seeke a battle as we are :
Nor as we are, we say we will not shun it.
   Herauld. I shall deliver so : thanks to your Majestie.
   Glos. My Liege, I hope they will not come upon us now.
   King. We are in Gods hand brother, not in theirs :
To night we will encampe beyond the bridge,
And on to morrow bid them march away.

Enter Burbon, Constable, Orleance, Gebon.

   Const. Tut I have the best armour in the world.
   Orleance. You have an excellent armour,
But let my horse have his due.
   Burbon. Now you talke of a horse, I have a steed like the
Palfrey of the sun, nothing but pure ayre and fire,
And hath none of this dull element of earth within him.

[61]

Orleance. He is of the colour of the Nutmeg.
Bur. And of the heate, a the Ginger.
Turne all the sands into eloquent tongues,
And my horse is argument for them all :
I once writ a Sonnet in the praise of my horse,
And began thus. Wonder of nature.
   Con. I have heard a Sonnet begin so,
In the praise of ones Mistresse.
   Burb. Why then did they immitate that
Which I writ in praise of my horse,
For my horse is my mistresse.
   Con. Ma foy the other day, me thought
Your mistresse shooke you shrewdly.
   Bur. I bearing me. I tell thee Lord Constable,
My mistresses weares her owne haire.
   Con. I could make as good a boast of that,
If I had had a sow to my mistresse.
   Bur. Tut thou wilt make use of any thing,
   Con. Yet I do not use my horse for my mistresse.
   Bur. Will it never be morning?
Ile ride too morrow a mile,
And my way shalbe paved with English faces.
   Con. By my faith so will not I,
For feare I be outfaced of my way.
   Bur. Well ile go arme my selfe, hay.
   Gebon. The Duke of *Burbon* longs for morning
   Or. I he longs to eate the English.
   Con. I thinketh heele eate all he killes.
   Orle. O peace, ill will never said well.
   Con. Ile cap that proverbe,
With there is flattery in friendship.
   Or. O Sir, I can answere that,
With give the divel his due.
   Con. Have at the eye of that proverbe,
With a Jogge of the divel.
   Or. Well the Duke of *Burbon*, is simply,
The most active Gentleman of *France*.

[62]

Con. Doing his activitie, and heele stil be doing.

Or. He never did hurt as I heard off.

Con. No I warrant you, nor never will.

Or. I hold him to be exceeding valiant.

Con. I was told so by one that knows him better then you.

Or. Whose that?

Con. Why he told me so himselfe :
And said he cared not who knew it.

Or. Well who will go with me to hazard,
For a hundred English prisoners?

Con. You must go to hazard your selfe,
Before you have them.

Enter a Messenger.

Mess. My Lords, the English lye within a hundred
Paces of your Tent.

Con. Who hath measured the ground?

Mess. The Lord *Granpeere.*

Con. A valiant man, a. an expert Gentleman.

Come, come away :
The Sun is hie, and we weare out the day.   *Exit omnes.*

Enter the King disguised, to him Pistoll.

Pist. Ke ve la?

King. A friend.

Pist. Discus unto me, art thou Gentleman?
Or art thou common, base, and popeler?

King. No sir, I am a Gentleman of a Company.

Pist. Trailes thou the puissant pike?

King. Even so sir. What are you?

Pist. As good a gentleman as the Emperour.

King. O then thou art better then the King?

Pist. The kings a bago, and a hart of gold.

Pist. A lad of life, an impe of fame :
Of parents good, of fist most valiant :
I kis his durtie shoe : and from my hart strings
I love the lovely bully. What is thy name?

[63]

King. Harry le Roy.

Pist. Le Roy, A Cornish man :
Art thou of Cornish crew?

Kin. No sir, I am a Wealchman.

Pist. A Wealchman : knowst thou *Flewellen*?

Kin. I sir, he is my kinsman.

Pist. Art thou his friend?

Kin. I sir.

Pist. Figa for thee then : my name is *Pistoll*.

Kin. It sorts well with your fiercenesse.

Pist. Pistoll is my name.

Exit Pistoll.

Enter Gower and Flewellen.

Gour. Captaine *Flewellen*.

Flew. In the name of Jesu speake lewer.
It is the greatest folly in the worell, when the auncient
Prerogatives of the warres be not kept.
I warrant you, if you looke into the warres of the Romanes,
You shall finde no tittle tattle, nor bible bable there :
But you shall finde the care, and the feares,
And the ceremonies, to be otherwise.

Gour. Why the enemy is loud : you heard him all night.

Flew. Godes sollud, if the enemy be an Asse & a Foole,
And a prating cocks-come, is it meet that we be also a foole,
And a prating cocks-come, in your coscience now?

Gour. Ile speake lower.

Flew. I beseech you do, good Captaine *Gower*.

Exit Gower, and Flewellen.

Kin. Tho it appeare a litle out of fashion,
Yet theres much care in this.

Enters three Souldiers

1. Soul. Is not that the morning yonder?

2. Soul. I we see the beginning.
God knowes whether we shall see the end or no.

[64]

3. Soul. Well I thinke the king could wish himselfe
Up to the necke in the middle of the Thames,
And so I would he were, at all adventures, and I with him.
  Kin. Now masters god morrow, what cheare?
  3. S. I faith small cheer some of us is like to have,
Ere this day ende.
  Kin. Why fear nothing man, the king is frolike,
  2. S. I he may be, for he hath no such cause as we
  Kin. Nay say not so, he is a man as we are.
The Violet smels to him as to us :
Therefore if he see reasons, he feares as we do.
  2. Sol. But the king hath a heavy reckoning to make,
If his cause be not good : when all those soules
Whose bodies shall be slaughtered here,
Shall joyne together at the latter day,
And say *I* dyed at such a place. Some swearing :
Some their wives rawly left :
Some leaving their children poore behind them.
Now if his cause be bad, I think it will be a greevous matter
                                              (to him.
  King. Why so you may say, if a man send his servant
As Factor into another Countrey,
And he by any meanes miscarry,
You may say the businesse of the maister,
Was the author of his servants misfortune.
Or if a sonne be imployd by his father,
And he fall into any leaud action, you may say the father
Was the author of his sonnes damnation.
But the master is not to answere for his servants,
The father for his sonne, nor the king for his subjects :
For they purpose not their deaths, when they crave their ser-
Some there are that have the gift of premeditated   (vices :
Murder on them :
Others the broken seale of Forgery, in beguiling maydens.
Now if these outstrip the lawe,
Yet they cannot escape Gods punishment.
War is Gods Beadel. War is Gods vengeance :

Every mans service is the kings :
But every mans soule is his owne.
Therfore I would have every souldier examine himselfe.
And wash every moath out of his conscience :
That in so doing, he may be the readier for death :
Or not dying, why the time was well spent,
Wherein such preparation was made.

   3. Lord. Yfaith he saies true :
Every mans fault on his owne head,
I would not have the king answere for me.
Yet I intend to fight lustily for him.

   King. Well, I heard the king, he wold not be ransomde.

   2. L. I he said so, to make us fight :
But when our throates be cut, he may be ransomde,
And we never the wiser.

   King. If I live to see that, Ile never trust his word againe.

   2. Sol. Mas youle pay him then, tis a great displeasure
That an elder gun, can do against a cannon,
Or a subject against a monarke.
Youle nere take his word again, your a nasse goe.

   King. Your reproofe is somewhat too bitter :
Were it not at this time I could be angry.

   2. Sol. Why let it be a quarrell if thou wilt.

   King. How shall I know thee?

   2. Sol. Here is my glove, which if ever I see in thy hat,
Ile challenge thee, and strike thee.

   Kin. Here is likewise another of mine,
And assure thee ile weare it.

   2. Sol. Thou dar'st as well be hangd.

   3. Sol. Be friends you fooles,
We have French quarrels anow in hand :
We have no need of English broyles.

   Kin. Tis no treason to cut French crownes,
For to morrow the king himselfe wil be a clipper,

Exit the souldiers.

[66]

Henry the fift

*Enter the King, Gloster, Epingam, and
Attendants.*

K. O God of battels steele my souldiers harts,
Take from them now the sence of reckoning,
That the apposed multitudes which stand before them,
May not appall their courage.
O not to day, not to day ô God,
Thinke on the fault my father made,
In compassing the crowne.
I *Richards* bodie have interred new,
And on it hath bestowd more contrite teares,
Then from it issued forced drops of blood :
A hundred men have I in yearly pay,
Which every day their withered hands hold up
To heaven to pardon blood.
And I have built rwo chanceries, more wil I do :
Tho all that I can do, is all too litle.

Enter Gloster.

Glost. My Lord.
King. My brother *Glosters* voyce.
Gloster. My Lord, the Army stayes upon your presence.
King. Stay *Gloster* stay, and I will go with thee,
The day my friends, and all thing, stayes for me.

Enter Clarence, Gloster, Exeter, and Salisburie.

War. My Lords the French are very strong.
Exe. There is five to one, and yet they all are fresh.
War. Of fighting men they have full fortie thousand.
Sal. The oddes is all too great. Farewell kind Lords :
Brave *Clarence*, and my Lord of *Gloster*,
My Lord of *Warwicke*, and to all farewell.
Clar. Farewell kind Lord, fight valiantly today,
And yet in truth, I do thee wrong,
For thou art made on the rrue sparkes of honour.

[67]

Enter King.

    War. O would we had but ten thousand men
Now at this instant, that doth not worke in England.
    King. Whose that, that wishes so, my Cousen *Warwick*?
Gods will, I would not loose the honour
One man would share from me,
Not for my Kingdome.
No faith my Cousen, wish not one man more,
Rather proclaime it presently through our campe,
That he that hath no stomacke to this feast,
Let him depart, his pasport shall bee drawne,
And crownes for convoy put into his purse,
We would not die in that mans company,
That feares his fellowship to die with us.
This day is called the day of Cryspin,
He that outlives this day, and sees old age,
Shall stand a tiptoe when this day is named,
And rowse him at the name of Cryspin.
He that outlives this day, and comes safe home,
Shall yearely on the vygill feast his friends,
And say, to morrow is S. Cryspines day :
Then shall we in their flowing bowles
Be newly remembred. *Harry* the King,
Bedford and *Exeter*, *Clarence* and *Gloster*,
Warwick and *Yorke*.
Familiar in their mouthes as houshold words.
This story shall the good man tell his sonne,
And from this day, unto the generall doome :
But we in it shall be remembred.
We fewe, we happie fewe, we bond of brothers,
For he to day that sheads his blood by mine,
Shalbe my brother : be he nere so base,
This day shall gentle his condition.
Then shall he strip his sleeves, and shew his skars,
And say, these wounds I had on Crispines day :
And Gentlemen in England now a bed,

Shall thinke themselves accurst,
And hold their manhood cheape,
While any speake that fought with us
Upon Saint Crispines day.

   Glost. My gracious Lord,
The French is in the field.

   Kin. Why all things are ready, if our minds be so.

   War. Perish the man whose mind is backward now.

   King. Thou dost not wish more help from England cousen?

   War. Gods will my Liege, would you and I alone,
Without more helpe, might fight this battle out.

   [King.] Why well said. That doth please me better,
Then to wish me one. You know your charge,
God be with you all.

Enter the Herald from the French.

   Herald. Once more I come to know of thee king *Henry*,
What thou wilt give for raunsome?

   Kin. Who hath sent thee now?

   Her. The Constable of *France*.

   Kin. I prethy beare my former answer backe :
Bid them atchieve me, and then sell my bones.
Good God, why should they mock good fellows
The man that once did sell the Lions skin,   (thus?
While the beast lived, was kild with hunting him.
A many of our bodies shall no doubt
Finde graves within your realme of *France* :
Tho buried in your dunghils, we shalbe famed,
For there the Sun shall greete them,
And draw up their honors reaking up to heaven,
Leaving their earthly parts to choke your clyme :
The smel whereof, shall breed a plague in *France* :
Marke then abundant valour in our English,
That being dead, like to the bullets crasing
Breakes forth into a second course of mischiefe,
Killing in relaps of mortailitie :
Let me speake proudly,

[69]

Ther's not a peece of feather in our campe,
Good argument I hope we shall not flye :
And time hath worne us into slovendry.
But by the mas, our hearts are in the trim,
And my poore souldiers tel me, yet ere night
Thayle be in fresher robes, or they will plucke
The gay new cloathes ore your French souldiers eares,
And turne them out of service. If they do this,
As if it please God they shall,
Then shall our ransome soone be levied.
Save thou thy labour Herauld :
Come thou no more for ransom, gentle Herauld.
They shall have nought I sweare, but these my bones :
Which if they have, as *I* wil leave am them,
Will yeeld them litle, tell the Constable.

    Her. *I* shall deliver so.

Exit Herauld.

    Yorke. My gracious Lord, upon my knee *I* crave,
The leading of the vaward.

    Kin. Take it brave *Yorke.* Come souldiers lets away :
And as thou pleasest God, dispose the day.

Exit.

Enter the foure French Lords.

    Ge. O diabello.
    Const. Mor du ma vie.
    Or. O what a day is this!
    Bur. O Jour die houte all is gone, all is lost.
    Con. We are inough yet living in the field,
To smother up the English,
If any order might be thought upon.

    Bur. A plague of order, once more to the field,
And he that will not follow *Burbon* now,
Let him go home, and with his cap in hand,
Like a bace leno hold the chamber doore,
Why least by a slave no gentler then my dog,

[70]

His fairest daughter is contamuracke.

   Con. Disorder that hath spoyld us, right us now,
Come we in heapes, weele offer up our lives
Unto these English, or else die with fame.

   Come, come along,
Lets dye with honour, our shame doth last too long.

Exit omnes.

Enter Pistoll, the French man, and the Boy.

   Pist. Eyld cur, eyld cur.
   French. O Monsire, je vous en pree aves petie de moy.
   Pist. Moy shall not serve. *I* will have fortie moys.
Boy aske him his name.
   Boy. Comant ettes vous appelles?
   French. Monsier *Fer.*
   Boy. He saies his name is Master *Fer.*
   Pist. *I*le Fer him, and ferit him, and ferke him :
Boy discus the same in French.
   Boy. Sir I do not know, whats French
For fer, ferit and fearkt.
   Pist. Bid him prepare, for I wil cut his throate.
   Boy. Feate, vou preat, il voulles coupele votre gage.
   Pist. Ony e ma foy couple la gorge.
Unlesse thou give to me egregious raunsome, dye.

One poynt of a foxe.

   French. Qui dit ill monsiere.
Ill ditye si vou ny vouly pa domy luy.
   Boy. La gran ransome, ill vou tueres.
   French. O Jee vous en pri pettit gentelhome, parle
A cee, gran captaine, pour avez mercie
A moy, ey Jee donerees pour mon ransome
Cinquante ocios. Je suyes ungentelhome de *France.*
   Pist. What sayes he boy?
   Boy. Marry sir he sayes, he is a Gentleman of a great
House, of *France* : and for his ransome,
He will give you 500. crownes.

Pist. My fury shall abate,
And I the Crownes will take.
And as I suck blood, I will some mercie shew.
Follow me cur.

Exit omnes.

Enter the King and his Nobles, Pistoll.

King. What the French retire?
Yet all is not done, yet keepe the French the field.
 Exe. The Duke of *Yorke* commends him to your Grace.
 King. Lives he good Unckle, twise I sawe him downe,
Twise up againe :
From helmet to the spurre, all bleeding ore.
 Exe. In which aray, brave souldier doth he lye,
Larding the plaines and by his bloody side,
Yoake fellow to his honour dying wounds,
The noble Earle of *Suffolke* also lyes.
Suffolke first dyde, and *Yorke* all hasted ore,
Comes to him where in blood he lay steept,
And takes him by the beard, kisses the gashes
That bloodily did yane upon his face,
And cryde aloud, tary deare cousin *Suffoke* :
My soule shall thine keep company in heaven :
Tary deare soule awhile, then flie to rest :
And in this glorious and well foughten field,
We kept togither in our chivaldry.
Upon these words I came and cheerd them up,
He tooke me by the hand, said deare my Lord,
Commend my service to my soveraigne.
So did he turne, and over *Suffolkes* necke
He threw his wounded arme, and so espoused to death,
With blood he sealed. An argument
Of never ending love. The pretie and sweet maner of it,
Forst those waters from me, which I would have stopt,
But I not so much of man in me,

[72]

But all my mother came into my eyes,
And gave me up to teares.
  Kin. I blame you not : for hearing you,
I must convert to teares.
      Alarum soundes.
What new alarum is this?
Bid every souldier kill his prisoner.
  Pist. Couple gorge.
           Exit omnes.

  Enter Flewellen, and Captaine Gower.

  Flew. Godes plud kil the boyes and the lugyge,
Tis the arrants peece of knavery as can be desired,
In the worell now, in your conscience now.
  Gour. Tis certaine, there is not a Boy left alive,
And the cowerdly rascals that ran from the battell,
Themselves have done this slaughter :
Beside, they have carried away and burnt,
All that was in the kings Tent :
Whereupon the king caused every prisoners
Throat to be cut. O he is a worthy king.
  Flew. I he was born at *Monmorth.*
Captain Gower, what call you the place where
Alexander the big was borne?
  Gour. Alexander the great.
  Flew. Why I pray, is nat big great?
As if I say, big or great, or magnanimous,
I hope it is all one reconing,
Save the frase is a litle varation.
  Gour. I thinke *Alexander the* great
Was borne at *Macedon.*
His father was called *Philip of Macedon*,
As *I* take it.
  Flew. I thinke it was *Macedon* indeed where *Alexander*
Was borne : looke you captaine *Gower*,
And if you looke into the mappes of the worell well,
You shall finde litle difference betweene

[73]

Macedon and *Monmorth*. Looke you, there is
A River in *Macedon*, and there is also a River
In *Monmorth*, the Rivers name at *Monmorth*,
Is called Wye.
But tis out of my braine, what is the name of the other :
But tis all one, tis so like, as my fingers is to my fingers,
And there is Samons in both.
Looke you captaine *Gower*, and you marke it,
You shall finde our King is come after *Alexander*.
God knowes, and you know, that *Alexander* in his
Bowles, and his alles, and his wrath, and his displeasures.
And indignations, was kill his friend *Clitus*.

   Gower. *I* but our King is not like him in that,
For he never killd any of his friends.

   Flew. Looke you, tis not well done to take the tale out
Of a mans mouth, ere it is made an end and finished :
I speake in the comparisons, as *Alexander* is kill
His friend *Clitus* : so our King being in his ripe
Wits and judgements, is turne away, the fat knite
With the great belly doublet : I am forget his name.

   Gower. Sir *John Falstaffe*.

   Flew. I, I thinke it is Sir John *Falstaffe* indeed,
I can tell you, theres good men borne at *Monmorth*.

Enter King and the Lords.

   King. I was not angry since *I* came into *France*,
Untill this houre.
Take a trumpet Herauld,
And ride unto the horsmen on yon hill :
If they will fight with us bid them come downe,
Or leave the field, they do offend our sight :
Will they do neither, we will come to them,
And make them skyr away, as fast
As stones enforst from the old Assirian slings.
Besides, weele cut the throats of those we have,
And not one alive shall taste our mercy.

Enter the Herauld.

Gods will what meanes this? knowst thou not
That we have fined these bones of ours for ransome?
    Herald. I come great king for charitable favour,
To sort our Nobles from our common men,
We may have leave to bury all our dead,
Which in the field lye spoyled and troden on.
    Kin. I tell thee truly Herauld, I do not know whether
The day be ours or not :
For yet a many of your French do keep the field.
    Hera. The day is yours.
    Kin. Praised be God therefore.
What Castle call you that?
    Hera. We call it *Agincourt.*
    Kin. Then call we this the field of *Agincourt.*
Fought on the day of *Cryspin, Cryspin.*
    Flew. Your grandfather of famous memorie,
If your grace be remembred,
Is do good service in *France.*
    Kin. Tis true *Flewellen.*
    Flew. Your Majestie sayes verie true.
And it please your Majestie,
The Wealchmen there was do good service,
In a garden where Leekes did grow.
And I thinke your Majestie wil take no scorne,
To weare a Leake in your cap upon S. *Davies* day.
    Kin. No *Flewellen*, for I am wealch as well as you.
    Flew. All the water in *Wye* wil not wash your wealch
Blood out of you, God keep it, and preserve it,
To his graces will and pleasure.
    Kin. Thankes good countryman.
    Flew. By Jesus I am your Majesties countryman :
I care not who know it, so long as your majesty is an honest
    K. God keep me so. Our Herald go with him,   (man
And bring us the number of the scattred French.

Exit Heralds.

Call yonder souldier hither.

    Flew. You fellow come to the king.

    Kin. Fellow why doost thou weare that glove in thy hat?

    Soul. And please your majestie, tis a rascals that swagard
With me the other day : and he hath one of mine,
Which if ever I see, I have sworne to strike him.
So hath he sworne the like to me.

    K. How think you *Flewellen*, is it lawfull he keep his oath?

    Fl. And it please your majesty, tis lawful he keep his vow.
If he be perjur'd once, he is as arrant a beggerly knave,
As treads upon too blacke shues.

    Kin. His enemy may be a gentleman of worth.

    Flew. And if he be as good a gentleman as Lucifer
And Belzebub, and the divel himselfe,
Tis meete he keepe his vowe.

    Kin. Well sirrha keep your word.
Under what Captain servest thou?

    Soul. Under Captaine *Gower.*

    Flew. Captaine *Gower* is a good Captaine :
And hath good littrature in the warres.

    Kin. Go call him hither.

    Soul. I will my Lord.

Exit souldier.

    Kin. Captain *Flewellen*, when *Alonson* and I was
Downe together, *I* tooke this glove off from his helmet,
Here *Flewellen*, weare it. If any do challenge it,
He is a friend of *Alonsons,*
And an enemy to mee.

    Fle. Your majestie doth me as great a favour
As can be desired in the harts of his subjects.
I would see that man now that should chalenge this glove :
And it please God of his grace, *I* would but see him,
That is all.

    Kin. Flewellen knowst thou Captaine *Gower*?

Fle. Captaine *Gower* is my friend.
And if it like your majestie, *I* know him very well.
   Kin. Go call him hither.
   Flew. I will and it shall please your majestie.
   Kin. Follow *Flewellen* closely at the heeles,
The glove he weares, it was the souldiers :
It may be there will be harme betweene them,
For I do know *Flewellen* valiant,
And being toucht, as hot as gunpowder :
And quickly will returne an injury.
Go see there be no harme betweene them.

Enter Gower, Flewellen, and the Souldier.

Flew. Captain *Gower*, in the name of Jesu,
Come to his Majestie, there is more good toward you,
Then you can dreame off.
   Soul. Do you heare you sir? do you know this glove?
   Flew. I know the glove is a glove.
   Soul. Sir I know this, and thus I challenge it.

He strikes him.

Flew. Gode plut, and his. Captain *Gower* stand away :
Ile give treason his due presently.

Enter the King, Warwicke, Clarence, and Exeter.

Kin. How now, what is the matter?
   Flew. And it shall please your Majestie,
Here is the notablest peece of treason come to light,
As you shall desire to see in a sommers day.
Here is a rascall, beggerly rascall, is strike the glove,
Which your Majestie tooke out the helmet of *Alonson* :
And your Majestie will beare me witnes, and testimony,
And avouchments, that this is the glove.
   Soul. And it please your Majestie, that was my glove.
He that I gave it too in the night,
Promised me to weare it in his hat :

[77]

I promised to strike him if he did.
I met that Gentleman, with my glove in his hat,
And I thinke I have bene as good as my word.

    Flew. Your Majestie heares, under your Majesties
Manhood, what a beggerly lowsie knave it is.

    Kin. Let me see thy glove. Looke you,
This is the fellow of it.
It was I indeed you promised to strike.
And thou thou hast given me most bitter words.
How canst thou make us amends?

    Flew. Let his necke answere it,
If there be any marshals lawe in the worell.

    Soul. My Liege, all offences come from the heart :
Never came any from mine to offend your Majestie.
You appeard to me as a common man :
Witnesse the night, your garments, your lowlinesse,
And whatsoever you received under that habit,
I beseech your Majestie impute it to your owne fault
And not mine. For your selfe came not like your selfe :
Had you bene as you seemed, I had made no offence.
Therefore I beseech your grace to pardon me.

    Kin. Unckle, fill the glove with crownes,
And give it to the souldier. Weare it fellow,
As an honour in thy cap, till I do challenge it.
Give him the crownes. Come Captaine *Flewellen*,
I must needs have you friends.

    Flew. By Jesus, the fellow hath metall enough
In his belly. Harke you souldier, there is a shilling for you,
And keep your selfe out of brawles & brables, & dissentions,
And looke you, it shall be the better for you.

    Soul. Ile none of your money sir, not I.

    Flew. Why tis a good shilling man.
Why should you be queamish? Your shoes are not so good :
It will serve you to mend your shoes.

    Kin. What men of sort are taken unckle?

    Exe. *Charles* Duke of *Orleance*, Nephew to the King.
John Duke of *Burbon*, and Lord *Bowchquall*.
Of other Lords and Barrons, Knights and Squiers,

Full fifteene hundred, besides common men.
This note doth tell me of ten thousand
French, that in the field lyes slaine.
Of Nobles bearing banners in the field,
Charles de le Brute, hie Constable of *France*.
Jaques of Chattillian, Admirall of *France*,
The Maister of the crosbows, *John* Duke *Alŏson*.
Lord *Ranbieres*, hie Maister of *France*.
The brave sir *Gwigzard, Dolphin*. Of *Nobelle Charillas*,
Gran *Prie*, and *Rosse*, *Fawconbridge* and *Foy*.
Gerard and *Verton*. *Vandemant* and *Lestra*.
Here was a royall fellowship of death.
Where is the number of our English dead?
Edward the Duke of *Yorke*, the Earle of *Suffolke*,
Sir *Richard Ketly, Davy Gam* Esquier :
And of all other, but five and twentie.
O God thy arme was here,
And unto thee alone, ascribe we praise.
When without strategem,
And in even shock of battle, was ever heard
So great, and litle losse, on one part and an other.
Take it God, for it is onely thine.
    Exe. Tis wonderfull.
    King. Come let us go on procession through the camp :
Let it be death proclaimed to any man,
To boast hereof, or take the praise from God,
Which is his due.
    Flew. *I*s it lawful, and it please your Majestie,
To tell how many is kild?
    King. Yes *Flewellen*, but with this acknowledgement,
That God fought for us.
    Flew. Yes in my conscience, he did us great good.
    King. Let there be sung, Nououes and te Deum.
The dead with charitie enterred in clay :
Weele then to *Calice*, and to England then,
Where nere from *France*, arrivde more happier men.

                    Exit omnes.

Enter Gower, and Flewellen.

Gower. But why do you weare your Leeke to day?
Saint *Davies* day is past?
    Flew. There is occasion Captaine *Gower*,
Looke you why, and wherefore,
The other day looke you, *Pistolles*
Which you know is a man of no merites
In the worell, is come where I was the other day,
And brings bread and sault, and bids me
Eate my Leeke : twas in a place, looke you,
Where *I* could move no discentions :
But if *I* can see him, *I* shall tell him,
A litle of my desires.
    Gow. Here a comes, swelling like a Turkecocke.

Enter Pistoll.

    Flew. Tis no matter for his swelling, and his turkecocks,
God plesse you Antient *Pistoll*, you scall,
Beggerly, lowsie knave, God plesse you.
    Pist. Ha, art thou bedlem?
Dost thou thurst base Troyan,
To have me folde up *Parcas* fatall web?
Hence, *I* am qualmish at the smell of Leeke.
    Flew. Antient *Pistoll*. I would desire you because
It doth not agree with your stomacke, and your appetite,
And you digestions, to eate this Leeke.
    Pist. Not for *Cadwalleder* and all his goates.
    Flew. There is one goate for you Antient Pistol.

He strikes him.

    Pist. Bace Troyan, thou shall dye.
    Flew. I, I know I shall dye, meane time, I would
Desire you to live and eate this Leeke.
    Gower. Inough Captaine, you have astonisht him.

Flew. Astonisht him, by *Jesu*, Ile beate his head
Foure dayes, and foure nights, but Ile
Make him eate some part of my Leeke.
   Pist. Well must I byte?
   Flew. I out of question or doubt, or ambiguities
You must byte.
   Pist. Good good.
   Flew. I Leekes are good, Antient *Pistoll*.
There is a shilling for you to heale your bloody coxkome.
   Pist. Me a shilling.
   Flew. If you will not take it,
I have an other Leeke for you.
   Pist. I take thy shilling in earnest of reconing.
   Flew. If I owe you any thing, ile pay you in cudgels,
You shalbe a woodmonger,
And by cudgels, God bwy you,
Antient *Pistoll*, God blesse you,
And heale your broken pate.
Antient *Pistoll*, if you see Leekes an other time,
Mocke at them, that is all : God bwy you.

                            Exit Flewellen.

   Pist. All hell shall stir for this.
Doth Fortune play the huswye with me now?
Is honour cudgeld from my warlike lines?
Well *France* farwell, newes have I certainly
That Doll is sicke. One mallydie of *France*,
The warres affordeth nought, home will I trug.
Bawd will I turne, and use the slyte of hand :
To England will I steale,
And there Ile steale.
And patches will I get unto these skarres,
And sweare I gat them in the Gallia warres.

                                Exit Pistoll.

[81]

The Chronicle Historie of

Enter at one doore, the King of England and his Lords. And at the other doore, the King of France, Queene Katherine, the Duke of Burbon, and others.

Harry. Peace to this meeting, wherefore we are met.
And to our brorher *France*, Faire time of day.
Faire health unto our lovely cousen *Katherine*.
And as a branch, and member of this stock :
We do salute you Duke of *Burgondie*.

Fran. Brother of *England*, right joyous are we to behold
Your face, so are we Princes English every one.

Duk. With pardon unto both your mightines.
Let it not displease you, if I demaund
What rub or bar hath thus far hindred you,
To keepe you from the gentle speech of peace?

Har. If Duke of *Burgondy*, you wold have peace,
You must buy that peace,
According as we have drawne our articles.

Fran. We have but with a cursenary eye,
Oreviewd them pleaseth your Grace,
To let some of your Counsell sit with us,
We shall returne our peremptory answere.

Har. Go Lords, and sit with them,
And bring us answere backe.
Yet leave our cousen *Katherine* here behind.

France. Withall our hearts.

Exit King and the Lords. Manet, Hrry, Katherine, and the Gentlewoman.

Hate. Now *Kate*, you have a blunt wooer here
Left with you.
If I could win thee at leapfrog,
Or with vawting with my armour on my backe,
Into my saddle,
Without brag be it spoken,
Ide make compare with any
But leaving that *Kate*,

[82]

If thou takest me now,
Thou shalt have me at the worst :
And in wearing, thou shalt have me better and better,
Thou shalt have a face that is not worth sun-burning.
But doost thou thinke, that thou and I,
Betweene Saint *Denis*,
And Saint *George*, shall get a boy,
That shall goe to *Constantinople*,
And take the great Turke by the beard, ha *Kate*?

    Kate. Is it possible that me sall
Love de enemie de *France*.

    Harry. No *Kate*, tis unpossible
You should love the enemie of *France* :
For *Kate*, I love *France* so well,
That Ile not leave a Village,
Ile have it all mine : then *Kate*,
When *France* is mine,
And I am yours,
Then *France* is yours,
And you are mine.

    Kate. I cannot tell what is dat.

    Harry. No *Kate*,
Why Ile tell it you in French,
Which will hang upon my tongue, like a bride
On her new married Husband.
Let me see, Saint *Dennis* be my speed.
Quan *France* et mon.

    Kate. Dat is, when *France* is yours.

    Harry. Et vous ettes amoy.

    Kate. And I am to you.

    Harry. Douck *France* ettes a vous :

    Kate. Den *France* sall be mine.

    Harry. Et Je suyues a vous.

    Kate. And you will be to me.

    Har. Wilt beleeve me *Kate*? tis easier for me
To conquer the kingdome, then to speak so much
More French.

Kate. A your Majesty has false *France* inough
To deceive de best Lady in *France.*

Harry. No faith *Kate* not I. But *Kate,*
In plaine termes, do you love me?

Kate. I cannot tell.

Harry. No, can any of your neighbours tell?
Ile aske them.
Come *Kate,* I know you love me.
And soone when you are in your closset,
Youle question this Lady of me.
But I pray thee sweete K*ate,* use me mercifully,
Because I love thee cruelly.
That I shall dye K*ate,* is sure :
But for thy love, by the Lord never.
What Wench,
A straight backe will growe crooked.
A round eye will growe hollowe.
A great leg will waxe small,
A curld pate prove balde :
But a good heart Kate, is the sun and the moone,
And rather the Sun and not the Moone :
And therefore K*ate* take me,
Take a souldier : take a souldier,
Take a King.
Therefore tell me K*ate,* wilt thou have me?

Kate. Dat is as please the King my father.

Harry. Nay it will please him :
Nay it shall please him K*ate.*
And upon that condition *Kate* Ile kisse you.

Ka. O mon du Je ne voudroy faire quelke chosse
Pour toute le monde,
Ce ne poynt votree fachion en fovor.

Harry. What saies she Lady?

Lady. Dat it is not de fasion en *France,*
For de maides, before da be married to
May foy je oblye, what is to bassie?

Har. To kis, to kis. O that tis not the

Fashion in *Frannce*, for the maydes to kis
Before they are married.
    Lady. Owye see votree grace.
    Har. Well, weele breake that custome.
Therefore *Kate* patience perforce and yeeld.
Before God *Kate*, you have witchcraft
In your kisses :
And may perswade with me more,
Then all the French Councell.
Your father is returned.

Enter the King of France, and
the Lordes.

How now my Lords?
    France. Brother of England,
We have orered the Articles,
And have agreed to all that we in sedule had.
    Exe. Only he hath not subscribed this,
Where your majestie demaunds,
That the king of *France* having any occasion
To write for matter of graunt,
Shall name your highnesse, in this forme :
And with this addition in French.
Nostre tresher filz, Henry Roy D'anglaterre,
E heare de France. And thus in Latin :
Preclarrisimus filius noster Henricus Rex Anglie,
Et heres Francie.
    Fran. Nor this have we so nicely stood upon,
But you faire brother may intreat the same.
    Har. Why then let this among the rest,
Have his full course : And withall,
Your daughter *Katherine* in mariage.
    Fran. This and what else,
Your majestie shall crave.
God that disposeth all, give you much joy.
    Har. Why then faire *Katherine*,
Come give me thy hand:

[85]

Our marriage will we present solemnise,
And end our hatred by a bond of love.
Then will I sweare to *Kate*, and *Kate* to mee :
And may our vowes once made, unbroken bee.

FINIS

Endnotes

Page 37

The Cronicle History: the play is based loosely on Raphael Holinshed's *Chronicles of England, Scotland, and Ireland* (1587). The term *History*, however, was regularly employed to denote a story, not one necessarily based on historical fact, of an exemplary kind.

Henry the fift (1387–1422), eldest son of Henry IV who had deposed Richard II. Tales of his wild youth followed by conversion to the model of Christian kingship were widely popular. During his father's reign he was active in suppressing internal rebellions and on his accession claimed the restoration of lands in France formerly held by English monarchs. His victory at Agincourt (1415) paved the way for the later Treaty of Troyes (1420) by which he married Katherine of Valois and was recognised as heir to the French throne. He died of dysentery at Bois de Vincennes during a third French campaign.

Auntient: a standard bearer or ensign.

Exeter: Thomas Beaufort (1390–1427), son of John of Gaunt and Henry's uncle.

2. Bishops: although not named, one must have represented the Archbishop of Canterbury, Henry Chichele (1362–1443), founder of All Souls College, Oxford (founded to commemorate the dead at Agincourt).

Clarence: Thomas, Duke of Clarence, Henry's brother.

Cousin: kinsman.

resolvde: freed from doubt.

touching us and France: concerning myself and the King of France.

become: grace.

Shure: sure.

[87]

proceed: debate, present the argument.

Lawe Salicke: A collection of folk customs and laws of no relevance to the succession which had become associated with Henry's claim to the throne of France. Henry derived his claim from the marriage of Philip IV's daughter, Isabella, to his great great grandfather Edward II. When, however, Isabella's elder brother Louis X had died in 1316, Isabella and her heirs had been debarred from the succession which had passed to the house of Valois.

fashion, frame, or wrest the same: i.e. pervert the argument in Henry's favour.

approbation: proving true.

impawne: pledge, commit, risk.

conjuration: solemn appeal.

note: give heed to.

sin: original sin.

Page 38

[*Bish.*]: The speech prefix is missing in the text but is anticipated by the catch phrase at the foot of the preceding page.

imperiall throne: Britain was often termed an empire in that it owed allegiance to no superior power and was itself comprised of separate but conjoined nation states.

Faramount: legendary king of the Franks.

gloze: gloss, interpret.

the flouds of Sabeck and of Elme: the rivers Saala and Elbe.

Charles the fift: Charlemagne.

dishonest maners: unchaste habits.

To wit: That is.

Mesene: Meissen, that territory between the Saala and Elbe mentioned above.

function: i.e. defunction or death.

Hugh Capet: founder of the Capetian dynasty.

fine: purify and complete (alluding to the legal term for a false conveyance).

Endnotes

Convaid: conveyed, dishonestly laid claim to (extending the legal terminology implicit in *fine* above).

Inger: in Holinshed, Lingard.

Charles: Charles the Bald.

So that as cleare as is the sommers Sun: This proverbial phrase often gives rise to laughter in the theatre. In the two most popular screen versions of the play, largely based on the Folio text, Olivier treats the debate comically and Branagh conspiratorially. The Quarto text gives less support to the charge that Henry goes to war on a flimsy pretext, but is sufficiently neutral to permit both readings.

King Pippins title: i.e. the claims of King Pepin I, the founder of the Carolingian dynasty.

King Charles his satisfaction: to satisfy Charles's conscience in regard to the legitimacy of his claim to the throne.

Page 39

And rather choose to hide them in a net: take refuge in an argument full of holes.

Then amply to imbace their crooked causes: than fully admit their illegitimate claims. (The argument of the French, if applied consistently, would debar their current and previous monarchs. *Imbace* is not found in *OED* and is a possible misreading of *embare* (reveal) or *embar* (invalidate).)

When the sonne dies, let the inheritance / Descend unto the daughter: cf. the passage cited by Holinshed from Numbers xxvii 8 – 'When a man dyeth & hath no sonne, ye shall turne his enheritance unto his daughter'.

bloody: portending bloodshed, blood-red.

great graunsirs: Edward III, Henry's grandfather.

ground: territory/theatre pit.

playd a Tragedy: the Battle of Crécy, extending the theatrical metaphor.

Making defeat on: defeating.

power: army.

his most mighty father: Edward III. The incident of Edward watching the Black Prince's exploits at Crécy from a nearby hill was recorded in Holinshed and popularised in the anonymous play of *Edward III*.

[89]

Endnotes

Foraging: preying.

entertaine: engage; but continuing the theatrical metaphor of 'playd a Tragedy' which is also implicit in the tone of 'smiling', 'behold', and 'laughing', within the passage.

cold for action: cold from lack of action.

onely: only.

But lay downe our proportion for the Scot: establish the proportion of our forces required to defend against the Scots.

rode: raid.

with all advantages: with everything in his favour.

The Marches: borderlands, with their own territorial armies.

guardyour: guard your.

coursing sneakers: hit and run raiders. The sport of coursing involves the hunting of hares by greyhounds.

the mayne entendement: hostile intention, full invasion by.

Unmaskt his power for France: invaded France.

never my great grandfather . . . But that the Scot: whenever my great grandfather . . . The Scots.

unfurnisht: ill equipped, unprepared.

breach: a break in a coast bay or harbour; but suggesting the military sense of a breach in defensive walls.

defences: troops.

brute: bruit, clamour, noise.

bin: been.

feared: alarmed.

Page 40
For heare her but examplified by her selfe: For note but the example of her own history.

chivalry: nobility, military leaders.

taken and impounded as a stray: captured and imprisoned (as though a stray animal in a pen).

Endnotes

the king of Scots: David II of Scotland was captured in 1346 while the main English army was in France. It was often incorrectly reported that he was then taken to Edward III at Calais.

caytiffe: prisoner, wretch.

owse: ooze.

wrack: wreckage.

shiplesse treasurie: sunken treasure.

If you will France win, / Then with Scotland first begin: The proverbial status of this view is confirmed by Holinshed and Hall.

in pray: in the act of preying (on France).

unfurnish: unguarded.

spoyle: plunder, destroy.

havock: lay waste.

curst: execrable, deserving of a curse.

advised: prudent.

For government though high or lowe, being put into parts, / Congrueth with a mutuall consent like musicke: The analogy between music and government was a commonplace of the period. The high pitched and low pitched parts, or melodies, combine mellifluously through consent, harmony of sounds.

the fate of man: the social station of the population.

divers functions: diverse, sundry, social roles.

but: butt, archery target.

by awe: through a natural recognition and reverence for divine authority.

Ordaine an act of order to a peopeld Kingdome: Decree ordered regulations for their hives. The analogy between the social hierarchy of the beehive and human society was a common place which goes back at least as far as Pliny's *Natural History* and was elaborated in Elyot's *The Governour*.

sort: different rank.

correct: administer correction.

venture: Overseas trade at this period was an extremely risky business (cf. venture capital).

Endnotes

Make boote: plunder.

pillage: honey.

busied in his majestie: fully occupied with his duties, but alluding to the greatness and glory of God.

behold: beholds.

Page 41

civell: civil, in the senses of civilian and well mannered.

sad eyde: sombre faced, with a possible suggestion of sorrowful.

executors: executioners, administrators of the law.

pale: frightful.

caning: F reads yawning.

one moment: the emphasis is not simply upon a single point in time but also the convergence of purpose.

losed severall wayes: loosed from several points.

close: converge.

dyall: sundial.

borne: sustained, born.

withall: as well.

Gallia: France.

pollicy and hardinesse: statesmanship and endurance.

from: Q reads frō.

Dolphin: the Dauphin Lewis, the Crown Prince of France, eldest son of Charles VI, who was not in fact present at Agincourt.

your: the assembled nobility.

awe: awesome power.

with full mouth: loudly.

Not worshipt with a paper Epitaph: without even the most short-lived memorial.

sparingly shew a farre off: discreetly hint at.

[92]

Endnotes

To whom our spirit is as subject, / As are our wretches fettered in our prisons:
We are as subject to the principles of Christian Kingship as prisoners are
to the power of the King.

Page 42

in fine: in short.

faith: in good faith.

Galliard: a quick, lively dance.

meeter: more appropriate.

tunne: cask or barrel.

Tennis balles: although the incident was popularly reported, there is no
historical evidence to support the fact that the Dauphin did send such an
insulting gift.

pleasant: merry.

matched: inaugurating a string of puns equating tennis to warfare. In Real
(or Royal) Tennis the leather ball was struck (matched) over a low net
spanning the court towards a narrow aperture, or hazard. The winning
point, or crown, is won when the ball becomes unplayable in the hazard.

wrangler: quarrelsome opponent.

chases: routs (punning on the tennis term for a ball which an opponent
has failed to return).

comes ore us: insults us.

seate: throne.

keepe our state: retain our royal dignity.

rowse us: awake, raise ourself.

this: i.e. to dazzle by contrast when crowned King of France.

lide: so Q, presumably in error for *like*.

I: Aye.

Page 43

balles: tennis balls; but punning on testicles.

gun stones: cannon balls.

wastefull: devastating.

Endnotes

flye from them: i.e. from the cannon balls.

comming: Q reads cōming.

collection: taxes and provisions for war (Q reads collectiō).

God before: with God before us, God willing.

on foote: afoot, in motion.

Nim and Bardolfe: both low-life companions of Hal and Falstaff in *1 & 2H4*.

Godmorrow: Good morning.

Nim: the name was slang for thief.

What: What (interrogative expletive).

antient: ancient, ensign.

wink: pretend to ignore the situation.

Iron: sword.

but what tho: but what of that.

toste: toast.

endure cold: i.e. when inactive (because not 'toasting cheese').

theres the humor of it: that's the melancholy truth of how I feel.

Page 44
Yfaith: In faith.

weart troth plight: were betrothed.

I must do as I may, tho patience be a tyred mare: the tiredness of mares was proverbial.

rest: conclusion (*rest* is a gaming term for reserve stake).

randevous: rendevous, refuge, last resort.

Pistoll and Hostes Quickly: further low-life characters from *Henry IV*.

Hoste: inn or lodging keeper, with an implication of pimp or low-class tavern keeper.

by gads lugges: by God's ears.

Endnotes

Nor shall my Nell keepe lodging: 'Hostess' was a common slang term for prostitute.

cannot: in Q printed *cānot*.

gentlewomen: printed as *gētlwomē* in Q.

by the prick of their needle: by embroidery, although the sexual quibble is obvious.

wilful adultry and murther: i.e. mayhem; wilful adultery is probably the Hostess's malapropism for rape.

the valour of a man, / And put up your sword: probably a comic malapropism rather than anything more profound.

Push: pish; a disdainful exclamation.

prickeard cur of Iseland: the prick-eared, long-haired lap-dogs of Iceland were noted for thick curly coats and snappish temperaments.

shog off: push off, go away.

solus: alone (perhaps also unmarried).

egregious: outrageous.

mesfull: dirty.

perdie: indeed, by God.

cock is up: blood is up, is cocked for firing.

Barbasom: a devil.

conjure: Pistol's outburst parodies the service of exorcism.

Page 45

And: if.

scoure you with my / Rapier: clean the barrel of your pistol with my sword.

furious wight: raging man.

gape: opens its jaws hungrily.

exall: draw (your sword).

mickle: much.

Couple gorge: *Couper la gorge*, French for 'cut the throat'.

Endnotes

the powdering tub of infamy: the tub where victims of venereal diseases were 'sweated'.

the lazar kite of Cresides kinde: Cressida was popularly reported to have been punished by the gods for her desertion of Troilus with leprosy, often considered a form of venereal disease at this time. Kite puns on cat (= whore) and cut (= cunt).

Doll Tear-sheete: a whore in *2H4*. Doll was a popular term for prostitute.

espowse: marry her.

quandom quickly: i.e. former Mistress Quickly.

For the onely she: For the only woman in the world.

Paco: referring to the latin, *pauca verba*, 'few words'.

my maister: my master (i.e. Falstaff).

do the office of a warming pan: alluding to Bardolph's alcohol inflamed complexion.

heele yeeld the crow a pudding one of these dayes: he'll be food for crows on the gallows (referring to the boy's lack of respect for his elders).

beating: betting.

Page 46

As manhood shall compound: the amount will be settled with swords.

Sword: punning on (God)'s word.

noble: a gold coin with a value of 6s 8d, rather less than the 8s Nim demands.

readie pay: pay up immediately.

combind: combine.

Is not thus just?: i.e. because Pistol will live by Nim (= thief), and Nim will live by Pistol who will be a Sutler, responsible for the provisions of war and notorious for dishonesty and profiteering.

occrue: accrue.

tashan contigian: probably another malapropism from Mistress Quickly. Contigian is probably derived from contagious and quotidian.

condoll: pass on our sympathies or condolences.

Gloster: Duke of Gloucester (1391–1447), the King's youngest brother.

Endnotes

I: Aye.

bedfellow: close friend (it was not unusual for men to share beds).

cloyed: surfeited.

forraine: foreign.

Lord of Massham: Henry, Baron Scroop of Masham, executed 1415.

Lord of Cambridge: Richard, Earl of Cambridge, second son of Edmund, Duke of York, executed 1415.

Page 47

my gentle Knight: Sir Thomas Grey, son-in-law to the Earl of Westmoreland, executed 1415.

Even those that were your fathers enemies: the treachery of Masham, Cambridge and Grey represented a stage of the continuing Yorkist opposition to the House of Lancaster.

galles: bitterness, thought to be derived from the gall bladder.

office: use. The sense of the line is obscured by the intrusive colon.

enlarge: free.

his more advice: on sober second thoughts.

securitie: over confidence.

orisons: prayers, pleas.

proceeding on distemper: committed under the influence of alcohol.

winked at: overlooked.

stretch our eye: express due astonishment.

capitall crimes: treasonable crimes punishable by death.

Chewed, swallowed and disgested: premeditated.

late Commissioners: recently appointed Commissioners (with authority to act in the King's name during his absence in France).

Page 48
bad: bade.

quit: perhaps in error for 'quick', alive.

Endnotes

English monsters: unnatural creatures (more unnatural by virtue of the fact that they are English rather than from some exotic source).

vilde: vile.

light crownes: worthless French coins.

Lightly: casually.

practises: plots.

Hampton: Southampton.

haah: hath, has.

counsell: confidences.

a coyned me into gold: Massham had served as Henry's Treasurer.

a practisde on: have intrigued against.

Page 49

annoy: hurt.

grose: gross.

open: open to view, apparent.

quit: acquit, pardon.

from: printed as *frō* in Q.

tender: tend, tenderly preserve.

successively: successful.

the signes of war advance: raise the battle standards.

Page 50

prethy: prithee, pray thee.

Stanes: Staines.

No fur: no further than here.

Arthors bosom: the Hostess muddles, to fine effect, the biblical Abraham ('the beggar died, and was carried by the angels into Abraham's bosom', Luke 16:22) with the legend of King Arthur.

crysombd childe: combining 'christened child' with 'crysom child', one dying within a month of birth.

Endnotes

Just at turning of the tide: referring to the folk belief that men were most likely to expire as the tide turned.

His nose was as sharpe as a pen: one of the traditional symptoms of approaching death.

floures: flowers.

upon: printed as *upō* in Q.

cride out on sack: railed against sack (Spanish wine to which Falstaff had been notoriously partial in *1 & 2H4*).

divels incarnat: devils in the flesh.

carnation: Quickly presumably misunderstands incarnat.

handle: speak of (with a sexual quibble).

rumaticke: rheumatic, feverish. The pronunciation (Romatic) suggested Rome and therefore the Roman Church, the protestants' 'Whore of Babylon', another scarlet woman.

That: his alcoholic complexion.

Page 51

Cleare up thy cristalles: wipe away your tears.

Looke to my chattels and my moveables: take good care of all my property.

pitch and pay: proverbial, cash payment only.

Mens words are wafer cakes: men's promises are thin and worthless.

And holdfast is the only dog my deare: perhaps proverbial (Brag is a good dog, but Holdfast is a better), but holdfast is also a clamp or miser, and dog a mechanical device for gripping. The sense would be, never give credit.

cophetua: so Q, alluding to Latin *coveto*, beware.

Keepe fast thy buggle boe: a bugle-bo is a bogy or wandering spirit. The term, however, also had a sexual sense and Pistol probably commands his wife to preserve her chastity.

s.d. King of France: King Charles VI (1368–1422), whose unstable mental health led to power struggles between the powerful Dukes of Burgundy and Orleans.

Endnotes

Bourbon: John, Duke of Bourbon, uncle to Charles VI, captured at Agincourt and died in captivity in 1433.

Orleance: Charles, Duke of Orleans (1391–1465), who married Richard II's widow, Isabella, and spent twenty-five years as an English captive after Agincourt.

Berry: John, Duke of Berri, member of Charles VI's Council, died 1416.

a Moris dance: Morris and other forms of folk dancing were widely regarded as frivolous, holiday activities.

idely: idly, frivolously.

Her scepter so fantastically borne: extending the image of the Morris dance, which could include a mock King and Queen.

humorous: capricious.

attends: accompanies.

Con: Constable of France, Charles de la Bret, the commander-in-chief of the French armies, killed at Agincourt.

late: recent.

Embassage: embassy, ambassador's message.

Page 52

cut up this English short: cut short the ambassador's interview.

devest: divest, strip off.

by gift of heaven, / Of lawe of nature, and of nations: Henry's claim is substantiated by divine authority, the authority of reason, and by legal precedent.

longs: belongs.

all wide stretched titles: all those titles deriving however remotely from the crown.

sinister: illegitimate (in heraldry, the bar sinister indicates bastardy).

awkeward: perverse.

rackte: raked.

these most memorable lynes: a document which sets out the lines of descent which justify Henry's claims.

Endnotes

branch: of the genealogical tree.

Willing: wishing.

overlooke: look over.

evenly derived: legitimately descended.

indirectly: dishonestly.

native: by right of birth (although paradoxically not a native of France).

challenger: claimant.

constraint: compulsion (Q reads cōstraint).

Page 53

requiring: requesting.

swallowed: consumed, destroyed.

prise: prize, value.

wombely vaultes: womb-like caverns.

second accent: echo.

oddes: strife.

Paris balles: tennis balls.

Lover: Louvre. The original spelling, Louer, puns on Louvre and Lover, an effect coarsened by the modernisation of v for u.

musters: exhibits (but glancing at the troops he now musters in France).

wayes: weighs.

Page 54

hie: hasten.

Godes plud: God's blood (in a stage Welsh accent).

Handkerchers: handkerchiefs.

fier shovell: coal shovel.

to carry coales: do dirty work, put up with insults.

Enter Gower: radical productions of the play tend to emphasise the fact that the officer class do not themselves storm the breach but remain in the rear of the fighting.

Endnotes

Gaptain: so Q, in error for Captain.

Mines: tunnels dug under enemy fortifications to lay explosives beneath the foundations.

concuavieties: concavities.

discusse: declare.

countermines: tunnels dug under those of the enemy.

Page 55

alarum: alarm, call to arms.

latest parley weele admit: the last truce or negotiation we will allow.

proud of destruction: glorying in the destruction of their city.

battery: assault.

halfe atchieved: half-conquered (implicitly linking military with sexual violation).

Harflew: Harfleur.

guiltie in defence: guilty because stubborn defiance in the face of overwhelming military power will lead to unnecessary destruction, and because the town owes 'true' allegiance to Henry, their 'rightful' King.

defensive: capable of defence.

Katherine: Katherine of Valois, daughter of Charles VI and, after her marriage to Henry, Queen of England. She subsequently married Owen Tudor and was great grandmother to Henry VIII.

parte: so Q, in error for *parle*, speak.

Alice venecia, vous aves cates en, / Vou parte fort bon Angloys englatara, / Coman sae palla vou la main en francoy: The scenes involving comic *Franglais* are difficult to annotate, presenting in all probability both deliberate and accidental error. The general sense, however, is clear and we provide translation of some of the key terms only.

main: French for hand.

Page 56

Le fot, e le con, ô Jesu! Je ne vew poinct parle, / Sie plus devant le che chevalires de franca, / Pur one million ma foy: Katherine recognises the sexual innuendo produced by her pronunciation of foot (= *foutre*, French for 'to fuck') and con (i.e. gown, but *con* in French is the equivalent to 'cunt'). The passage contains other sexual puns: nick was slang for 'vulva', as was the bo of ilbo and bilbo.

Some: the river Somme, between Harfleur and Calais.

Mordeu ma via: perhaps *Mort Dieu, ma vie!*, or *Mort de ma vie!*

spranes: sprays, offshoots (i.e. the English are merely bastard offspring of Norman French ancestors).

emptying: outpourings, dregs.

our fathers luxerie: forefathers' lust.

grafters: original stock.

mor du: *Mort Dieu*, God's death.

unfoughtwithall: unfought in addition.

nooke Ile: remote isle.

mettall: mettle.

Page 57

barley broath: barley broth (i.e. ale).

a drench for swolne Jades: a medical draught for diseased horses.

sodden water: boiled water (i.e. ale).

decockt: warm, infused.

quick: lively.

spirited: animated.

Iicesickles: icicles.

they a more frosty clymate: they from a more frosty climate.

Sweate drops of youthfull blood: i.e. from the exertions of warfare.

dispatch: go quickly.

Montjoy: title of the chief Herald of France.

Rone: Rouen. Historically, the Dauphin was not present at Agincourt; despite this exchange he nevertheless appears at the fictional battle without further comment.

from: printed *frō* in Q.

Endnotes

the bridge: Henry's troops established a bridgehead across the river Ternoise on the night before Agincourt.

excellent: printed *excellēt* in Q.

committed: printed as *cōmitted* in Q.

yᵉ: the.

man: printed as *mā* in Q.

livings: possessions.

worell: world (stage Welsh).

maintain: defend.

a man of no reckoning: of inferior social class.

ancient Pistoll: this seems inconsistent with his character elsewhere, but perhaps Pistol's bluster takes in friend and foe alike.

Page 58
I: aye.

buxsome: blithe, lively.

furious: cruel.

That Godes blinde: Fortune as a blind goddess standing upon a rolling rock was common emblem.

Plind: blind.

mufler: blindfold (allegorically the blindfold within the painting represents Fortune's blindness, although only a sighted person would need a blindfold).

Fortune is turning: both turning the wheel, and herself being whirled around.

her fate: both the fate of others which she controls, and her own destiny.

roules: rolls.

is make: is making.

excellent description: printed as *excellēt descriptiō* in Q.

and: an.

morall: symbolic figure.

packs: pax (tablet stamped with a crucifix).

Endnotes

let gallowes gape for dogs: cats and dogs were sometimes hanged for 'animal crimes'.

his windpipe stop: at this period hanging meant death through the drawn out and barbaric process of strangulation.

doome: judgement.

of pettie price: not justifying the death penalty, hardly worth stealing.

vitall threed: alluding to the thread of life which in classical mythology the Fates wove, measured and finally cut.

With edge of penny cord: by the hangman's rope.

approach: perhaps in error for 'reproach' (as in F), but if applied to the rope the sense 'advance of an enemy' is appropriate.

require: requite.

I partly understand your meaning: I understand your general drift. Pistol may be offering a bribe or there may be a joke at the expense of Pistol's rhetorical excess.

Page 59

figa . . . The figge of Spaine within thy Jawe: a contemptuous gesture which consisted in thrusting the thumb between two of the closed fingers or into the mouth. The modern equivalent would be 'fuck off' accompanied by a V sign.

maw: stomach.

lighten: lightning.

bawd: pimp.

heeis utter as prave words: he did utter such brave words.

gull: stupid person.

perfect: word-perfect.

sconce: fort, earthwork.

came off: acquitted himself.

stood on: insisted on.

con: learn.

in phrase of warre: in the jargon of battle.

Endnotes

trick up: dress.

new tuned: newly coined.

what a berd / Of the Generalls cut: wearing a beard in the fashion of the General (in the 1590s Essex set the fashion, which presumably Pistol followed on stage, for long, square beards).

horid: fearsome.

know: recognise.

slaunders of this age: one who brings disgrace to this age.

mistooke: mistaken, taken in.

Page 60

partition: casualties.

whelkes and knubs: pimples and lumps.

pumples: pustules.

his breath blowes at his nose: his breath fans the coal-red glow of his nose.

plew: blue.

his nose is executed, & his fire out: perhaps Bardolph's nose was slit, as was the custom, in the pillory prior to execution, but the fires of his nose would have been extinguished in any event by death.

abraided: upbraided, insulted.

lenitie: lenience.

habit: costume.

then: printed as *thē* in Q.

Advantage: the military advantage of superior numbers and preparation.

kue: cue.

admire our sufferance: wonder at our forbearance (in not attacking earlier).

Which to raunsome, / His pettinesse would bow under: Henry is too poor to be able to pay a ransom commensurate with the injuries he has occasioned.

effusion: spillage.

qualitie: profession.

faire: becomingly, justly.

Endnotes

impeach: hindrance.

Callis: Calais.

sooth: truth.

of craft and vantage: of power and advantage.

lessoned: lessened.

heire: punning on air and heir.

God before: with God leading us, God willing.

there is for your paines: presumably offering a reward.

Palfrey of the sun: in classical mythology the sun's chariot was drawn across the sky by fiery horses.

pure ayre and fire: air and fire were considered the noblest of the four elements, earth and water the basest.

Page 62

a the Ginger: of ginger.

argument: subject, theme.

Ma foy: indeed yes.

shrewdly: severely, shrewishly.

bearing: carrying (but throughout this passage there are puns on the sexual sense of mistress).

My mistresse weares her owne haire: baldness was one of the symptoms of venereal disease.

outfaced: driven from, shamed out of.

hay: an exclamation made when hitting an opponent, here in anticipation of battle.

Have at: a phrase announcing a hostile attack.

the eye: the bull's eye.

a Jogge of the divel: this proverb remains unknown and may be an error for 'a fig for the devil' (see 'fig' above).

active: energetic, lively.

[107]

Endnotes

Doing: with obscene sexual innuendo.

then: printed as *thē* in Q.

hazard: punning on wager/put in danger.

Ke ve la?: Qui va là? Who goes there?

Discus: declare.

Gentleman: one of gentle birth, properly one who is entitled to bear arms although not of the nobility.

popeler: popular, i.e. common.

Gentleman of a Company: gentleman volunteer, exempt from normal military discipline.

Trailes thou the puissant pike?: are you in the infantry? The pike was a favourite weapon of the English infantry and was carried when not in use with the butt trailing on the ground.

the Emperour: the Holy Roman Emperor.

bago: bawcock, i.e. fine fellow.

a hart of gold: 'a heart of gold' was a fairly common phrase for 'perfect fellow'.

Pist.: the redundant speech prefix is as in Q.

impe: (mischievous) child.

hart strings: the tendons or nerves supposed to brace and sustain the heart.

bully: familiar term of affection, 'fine fellow'.

le Roy: Le Roi, the King.

Page 64

crew: band of soldiers (but a Cornish crew was also a hovel or pigsty).

sorts: agrees.

lewer: lower.

Prerogatives: principles.

warrant: assure.

bible bable: bibble babble (equivalent to tittle tattle).

Endnotes

cares: precautions.

Godes sollud: an oath – God's lid (eyelid).

cocks-come: coxcomb, i.e. fool.

Page 65

at all adventures: at any event, anyhow.

frolike: merry.

reckoning: account of his conduct.

the latter day: the Day of Judgement.

rawly left: left unprovided for.

Factor: agent.

miscarry: perish.

author: cause.

leaud: lewd.

purpose: intend, plan.

when: printed as *whē* in Q.

gift: probably in error for guilt.

the broken seale of Forgery, in beguiling maydens: the broken seals are probably the seals of the marriage covenant, but with an allusion to sexual violation.

outstrip: escape.

Beadel: an officer who whipped criminals.

Page 66

moath: mote.

s.p. 3. Lord: the change from Souldier to Lord is confusing but merely emphasises the representative nature of those in conversation with Henry.

Mas: By the Mass.

pay him: pay him out.

elder gun: pop-gun (made from hollowed out elder wood).

anow: enough.

Endnotes

to cut French crownes: clip gold coins (a treasonable offence), cut off the heads of Frenchmen, seize the crown of France.

Epingam: Sir Thomas Erpingham (1357–1428), who ordered the English battle-line at Agincourt.

Page 67

sence of reckoning: ability to count (but also 'moral qualms').

apposed multitudes: opposing multitudes (but also the juxtaposition of the numbers within each army).

appall: dismay, terrify.

the fault my father made: Henry's father, Bolingbroke, had deposed Richard II and ordered his murder in Pomfret Castle.

compassing: grasping, machinating for.

interred new: Henry had Richard's remains reburied within Westminster Abbey. He endowed two religious houses but they do not seem to have sung masses for Richard's soul.

rwo: so Quarto, clearly in error for two.

stayes upon: attends upon, awaits.

Salisburie: Thomas Montacute, Earl of Salisbury (1388–1428), noted military leader later killed at the siege of Orleans.

yet: as yet.

War: Richard Beauchamp, Earl of Warwick (1381–1439) was for a time Regent of England during the minority of Henry VI.

rrue: probably in error for true.

Page 68

pasport: permit of discharge.

convoy: transport.

That feares his fellowship to die with us: that fears to die in our fellowship.

the day of Cryspin: 25 October, the feast of Crispinus and Crispianus, the patron saints of shoemakers.

the vygill: the night before.

Endnotes

Bedford: Duke of Bedford; Henry's younger brother, John of Lancaster (1390–1435).

Yorke: Duke of York; Aumerle (*c.* 1373–Agincourt), brother to the Earl of Cambridge, features in Shakespeare's *Richard II* and had been pardoned for treason by Henry IV.

good man: alluding to goodman, a yeoman or householder.

the generall doome: the Day of Judgement.

bond: fellowship.

gentle: ennoble.

Page 69
backward: lacking enthusiasm for battle.

from: printed as *frō* in Q.

[King.]: speech prefix missing in Q, but anticipated by the catchphrase at the foot of the preceding page.

one: completely alone.

charge: responsibility, command.

prethy: pray thee.

atchieve: capture.

The man that once did sell the Lions skin: alluding to Aesop's Fable of the hunter who sold a bearskin to a countryman before capturing the beast. The lion is an appropriately royal substitute.

honors: the sun will draw up not only the reeking stench of decaying flesh but the spiritual honour of the fallen soldier.

clyme: climate, territory.

crasing: fragmenting, ricocheting.

Killing in relaps of mortailitie: causing death to their enemies even while they relapse into the grave.

Page 70
Ther's not a peece of feather in our campe: in contrast to the gaudy apparel and frivolous attitude of the French.

slovendry: slovenliness.

Endnotes

in the trim: finely dressed, in good shape.

Thayle be in fresher robes: because in heaven (but perhaps the following *or* should be interpreted as *for*).

turne them out of servive: strip them of their livery, as though they were dismissed servants.

am: 'em.

vaward: vanguard.

Mor du ma vie: probably *Mort de ma vie!*

houte: probably in error for *honte*.

order: disciplined counterattack.

bace leno: base pander.

Page 71

Why least: whilst.

gentler: better born, more tender.

contamuracke: so Q, probably in error for contaminated.

eyld: probably in error for yield.

Fer: OED gives this as example of a meaningless verb.

ferit: ferret, hunt after, worry.

ferke: beat, whip.

egregious: great, significant.

One poynt of a foxe: on the point of a sword (since swords made in Germany were stamped with the sign of a fox).

Page 72

suck blood: extract cash.

Larding: lubricating with his blood.

Yoake fellow to his honour dying wounds: similarly mortally afflicted with honourable wounds.

all hasted ore: rushing over (but suggesting also the flowing blood from his wounds).

yane: yawn.

Endnotes

these: Q inverts the initial *t*.

cheerd them up: comforted them.

espoused: the image links the blood of battle with the blood of the broken hymen.

pretie and sweet: fine and pleasing.

Page 73

my mother: tears (springing from the tender, feminine side of his nature but alluding also to *the mother*, a term for hysteria).

alarum: alarm, signal calling men to arms.

plud: blood.

lugyge: perhaps those left to defend the baggage.

arrants: most arrant.

Whereupon: as the audience has just heard the order to kill the prisoners given before Henry learns of the slaughter of the boys, the conjunction does not seem to imply cause and effect, but rather attempts to justify Henry's action in relation to the barbarity of the French. Clearly his officers approve of Henry's 'righteous anger'.

reconing: reckoning, meaning (but punning on reckoning as *account*).

litle varation: minor rhetorical variation.

at Macedon: in fact Alexander was born at Pella, a town in Macedonia.

Page 74

Samons: salmon.

is come after: resembles.

Alexander in his / Bowles, and his alles, and his wrath: Alexander killed his general and close friend Cleitus during a bout of drunkenness.

For he never killd any of his friends: the phrase is given ironic point by the fact that at the end of the play all Henry's old friends from his tavern days are dead, with Bardolf executed as a result of his direct order.

turne away: 2H4.

great belly doublet: a stuffed doublet, but no doubt also referring to Falstaff's girth.

[113]

Endnotes

skyr: scurry.

enforst: violently thrown.

Page 75
fined: defined, agreed to pay as a ransom.

Cryspin, Cryspin: of Saint Crispin and his brother Saint Crispianus.

grandfather of famous memorie: presumably Henry's great grandfather, Edward III, victor at the battle of Crécy.

In a garden where Leekes did grow: although the exact incident remains unexplained the wearing of leeks is traditionally associated with Welsh nationalism.

Page 76
And: if it.

swagard: quarrelled.

sirrha: term of address assuming authority.

hath good littrature in the warres: has a sound knowledge of military theory and textbooks.

Page 77
toucht: angered (but alluding to touch-paper).

hot: violent.

know: acknowledge, recognise (although Flewellen misconstrues the meaning).

Gode plut: God's blood!

avouchments: assurances.

Page 78
thy glove: the glove he wears in his cap, earlier given to him by Henry.

thou thou: so Q.

marshals lawe: martial law.

metall: mettle.

brables, & dissentiōs: altercations and violent disputes (Q prints *dissentiōs*).

sort: note, rank.

Endnotes

Bowchquall: Boucicault.

Chattillian: Chatillon.

Ranbieres: Ramberes.

Gwigzard, Dolphin: Guichard, Dauphin.

Earle of Suffolke: Michael de la Pole, Earl of Suffolk (b. 1394).

Sir Richard Ketly: in Holinshed Kikely.

Davy Gam Esquier: David Ap Llewellyn of Brecon, called Gam (i.e. squinting).

strategem: trickery.

even: equal, fair.

Nououes: so Q in error for *Non nobis*.

more happier: more-happier.

sault: salt.

scall: scab (scall was a scaly or scabby disease of the scalp).

bedlem: insane (the Bethlehem Hospital housed the insane).

Troyan: Trojan (slang for someone of low character).

folde up Parcas fatall web: kill you. In classical mythology the Parcae were the three Fates who spun, wove and finally cut the thread of a man's life.

Hence: Away!

Cadwalleder: a seventh-century King of Wales and the last of the British Kings.

and all his goates: derisively associating Wales with goats.

astonisht: stunned.

coxkome: head, by association with the fool's cap.

in earnest of reconing: as downpayment for compensation or revenge.

cudgels: wooden clubs.

Endnotes

woodmonger: timber merchant.

by: buy.

God bwy you: God be with you.

huswye: hussy, strumpet.

lines: loins.

That Doll is sicke: there is almost certainly confusion of name and character here in both Q and F. Pistoll is married to Mistress Quickly, not the prostitute Doll Tearsheet.

mallydie of France: i.e. venereal disease.

trug: trudge (also a cant term for prostitute).

Gallia: Gallic, French.

Page 82

wherefore: the reason why.

brorher: so Q in error for brother, i.e. fellow monarch.

Duke of Burgondie: Philip the Good (1396–1467), Duke of Burgundy. The Houses of Burgundy and Orleans were rivals for power during the unstable reign of Charles VI and in 1419 Philip's father, John the Fearless, was murdered at the instigation of the Dauphin. As a consequence Philip supported Henry's campaign.

so are we Princes English every one: as we are to behold all the English princes.

rub: obstacle.

cursenary: cursory.

pleaseth: May it please.

peremptory: decisive, final.

cousen: a courtesy relationship since she is the daughter of a 'brother' King.

Hrry: so Q in error for Harry.

Manet: remain on stage.

Hate: so Q in error for Harry.

leapfrog: with obvious sexual innuendo.

vawting: vaulting.

Page 83

a face that is not worth sun-burning: one that is already ugly and cannot be further damaged from exposure to the sun (sun tans were unfashionable in the period).

Betweene Saint Denis, / And Saint George: the patron saints of France and England, who died *c.* 280 and *c.* 303 respectively.

That shall goe to Constantinople, / And take the great Turke by the beard: the recapture of Constantinople from the Turks (who captured the city in 1453, thirty-one years after the death of Henry V) was a major foreign policy aim of the rulers of sixteenth-century Christian Europe. Ironically, the son of Henry and Kate was the ineffectual Henry VI, who contrived to lose both the crowns of France and England.

Douck: presumably in error for Donck, then.

then: printed as *thē* in Q.

graunt: the granting of lands or titles.

nicely: scrupulously, foolishly.

present: immediately, in person.

Appendix

The Chronicle Hiſtorie

of *Henry* the fift : with his battel fought
at *Agin Court* in *France.*   Togither with
Auncient *Pistoll.*

[I. 2] *Enter King* Henry, Exeter, 2. *Biſhops* Clarence, *and other
Attendants.*

Exeter.

SHall I call in Thambaſſadors my Liege ?
　　King. Not yet my Couſin, til we be reſolude
　Of ſome ſerious matters touching vs and *France.*
4　　*Bi.* God and his Angels guard your ſacred throne,
　And make you long become it.
　　King. Shure we thank you. And good my Lord proceed
　Why the Lawe S*alicke* which they haue in *France,*
8 Or ſhould or ſhould not, ſtop vs in our clayme :
　And God forbid my wife and learned Lord,
　That you ſhould faſhion, frame, or wreſt the ſame.
　For God doth know how many now in health,
12 Shall drop their blood in approbation,
　Of what your reuerence ſhall incite vs too.
　Therefore take heed how you impawne our perſon,
　How you awake the ſleeping ſword of warre :
16 We charge you in the name of God take heed.
　After this coniuration, ſpeake my Lord :
　And we will iudge, note, and beleeue in heart,
　That what you ſpeake, is waſht as pure
20 As ſin in baptiſme.

　　　　　　　　　　　A 2　　　　　　　*Biſh.*

Then heare me gracious foueraigne, and you peeres,   [I. 2]
Which owe your liues, your faith and feruices
To this imperiall throne.
There is no bar to ftay your highneffe claime to *France*   24
But one, which they produce from *Faramount*,
No female fhall fucceed in falicke land,
Which falicke land the French vniuftly gloze
To be the realme of *France :*   28
And *Faramont* the founder of this law and female barre :
Yet their owne writers faithfully affirme
That the land falicke lyes in *Germany,*
Betweene the flouds of *Sabeck* and of *Elme,*   32
Where *Charles* the fift hauing fubdude the Saxons,
There left behind, and fetled certaine French,
Who holding in difdaine the Germaine women,
For fome difhoneft maners of their liues,   36
Eftablifht there this lawe.   To wit,
No female fhall fucceed in falicke land :
Which falicke land as I faid before,
Is at this time in *Germany* called *Mefene :*   40
Thus doth it well appeare the falicke lawe
Was not deuifed for the realme of *France,*
Nor did the French poffeffe the falicke land,
Vntill 400. one and twentie yeares   44
After the function of king *Faramont,*
Godly fuppofed the founder of this lawe :
Hugh Capet alfo that vfurpt the crowne,
To fine his title with fome fhowe of truth,   48
When in pure truth it was corrupt and naught :
Conuaid himfelfe as heire to the Lady *Inger,*
Daughter to *Charles,* the forefaid Duke of *Lorain,*
So that as cleare as is the fommers Sun,   52
King *Pippins* title and *Hugh Capets* claime,
King *Charles* his fatisfaction all appeare,
To hold in right and title of the female :
So do the Lords of *France* vntil this day,   56
Howbeit they would hold vp this falick lawe

                                    To

[I. 2] To bar your highneſſe claiming from the female,
  And rather chooſe to hide them in a net,
60 Then amply to imbace their crooked cauſes,
  Vſurpt from you and your progenitors. (claime ?
   K. May we with right & conſcience make this
   Bi. The ſin vpon my head dread foueraigne.
64 For in the booke of Numbers is it writ,
  When the ſonne dies, let the inheritance
  Deſcend vnto the daughter.
  Noble Lord ſtand for your owne,
68 Vnwinde your bloody flagge,
  Go my dread Lord to your great graunſirs graue,
  From whom you clayme :
  And your great Vncle *Edward* the blacke Prince,
72 Who on the French ground playd a Tragedy
  Making defeat on the full power of *France,*
  Whileſt his moſt mighty father on a hill,
  Stood ſmiling to behold his Lyons whelpe,
76 Foraging blood of French Nobilitie.
  O Noble Engliſh that could entertaine
  With halfe their Forces the full power of *France :*
  And let an other halſe ſtand laughing by,
80 All out of worke, and cold for action.
   King. We muſt not onely arme vs againſt the French,
  But lay downe our proportion for the Scot,
  Who will make rode vpon vs with all aduantages.
84 *Bi.* The Marches gracious foueraigne, ſhalbe ſufficient
  To guardyour *England* from the pilfering borderers.
   King. We do not meane the courſing ſneakers onely,
  But feare the mayne entendement of the Scot,
88 For you ſhall read, neuer my great grandfather
  Vnmaskt his power for *France,*
  But that the Scot on his vnfurniſht Kingdome,
  Came pouring like the Tide into a breach,
92 That *England* being empty of defences,
  Hath ſhooke and trembled at the brute hereof.
   Bi. She hath bin then more feared then hurt my Lord :

      A 3   Foɪ

For heare her but examplified by her selfe,
When all her chiualry hath bene in *France*   96
And she a mourning widow of her Nobles,
She hath her selfe not only well defended,
But taken and impounded as a stray, the king of Scots,
Whom like a caytiffe she did leade to *France*,   100
Filling your Chronicles as rich with praise
As is the owse and bottome of the sea
With sunken wrack and shiplesse treasurie.

   Lord. There is a saying very old and true,   104
If you will *France* win,
Then with *Scotland* first begin :
For once the Eagle, England being in pray,
To his vnfurnish nest the weazel Scot   108
Would suck her egs, playing the mouse in absence of the
To spoyle and hauock more then she can eat.   (cat :
   Exe. It followes then, the cat must stay at home,
Yet that is but a curst necessitie,   112
Since we haue trappes to catch the petty theeues :
Whilste that the armed hand doth fight abroad
The aduised head controlles at home :
For gouernment though high or lowe, being put into parts,   116
Congrueth with a mutuall consent like musicke.
   Bi. True : therefore doth heauen diuide the fate of man
           in diuers functions.
Whereto is added as an ayme or but, obedience :
For so liue the honey Bees, creatures that by awe   120
Ordaine an act of order to a peopeld Kingdome :
They haue a King and officers of sort,
Where some like Magistrates correct at home :
Others like Marchants venture trade abroad :   124
Others like souldiers armed in their stings,
Make boote vpon the sommers veluet bud :
Which pillage they with mery march bring home
To the tent royall of their Emperour,   128
Who busied in his maiestie, behold
The singing masons building roofes of gold :

                               The